ESSENTIAL READER

ESSENTIAL READING

ESSENTIAL READER

Sarojini Naidu

INTRODUCTION BY
MAKARAND R. PARANJAPE

EBURY
PRESS

An imprint of Penguin Random House

EBURY PRESS

USA | Canada | UK | Ireland | Australia
New Zealand | India | South Africa | China | Singapore

Ebury Press is part of the Penguin Random House group of companies
whose addresses can be found at global.penguinrandomhouse.com

Published by Penguin Random House India Pvt. Ltd
4th Floor, Capital Tower 1, MG Road,
Gurugram 122 002, Haryana, India

Penguin
Random House
India

First published in Ebury Press by Penguin Random House India 2022

Introduction copyright © Makarand R. Paranjape 2022
Selection and editorial matter copyright © Penguin Random House India 2022

ISBN 9780143454144

Typeset in Sabon by Manipal Technologies Limited, Manipal

Printed at Manipal Technologies Limited, India

www.penguin.co.in

MIX
Paper | Supporting
responsible forestry
FSC® C043100

This is a legitimate digitally printed version of the book and therefore might not
have certain extra finishing on the cover.

Contents

SPEECHES

LETTERS

Introduction

The Essential Sarojini Naidu? What would one include under such a title? To me it would be everything she wrote. That is because Sarojini wrote precious little. Apart from juvenilia, just three collections of verse, *The Golden Threshold* (1905), *The Bird of Time* (1912) and *The Broken Wing* (1917). A fourth, *The Feather of the Dawn* (1961), was published posthumously by her daughter, Padmaja. Also, a collection of speeches, based on transcripts not always properly edited, was published by G.A. Natesan of Madras, one of India's leading nationalist publishers, the revised third edition of which came out in 1925. The total corpus of her published work is, thus, quite compact, compared to her more famous and prolific contemporaries, such as Mahatma Gandhi or Jawaharlal Nehru, both of whom she knew and worked closely with.

But such is the paradox of history, that Sarojini Naidu (1879–1949), despite her meagre output, was world-famous at a very young age. She went on to become a living legend and one of the foremost national leaders of India. Somewhat of a child prodigy, she began writing

English verse at the age of eleven.* The following year, not yet in her teens, she passed the Madras Matriculation, which some say was harder than today's MA, at the age of twelve. At thirteen, she wrote 'Mehir Muneer', a long poem based on a Persian romance. At fifteen she fell in love with an older widower, Dr M. Govindarajulu Naidu, who belonged to a different caste. At sixteen she was India's first undergraduate student at Girton, the only women's college at Cambridge. Soon, she came in contact with the prominent poets of the fin-de-siècle as a regular invitee at Edmund Gosse's salon in London. She also met W.B. Yeats there.

Still in her teens, she returned to India without taking a degree. Girton, intended to produce sturdy nurses and teachers, did not suit a girl of her dreamy bent of mind and delicate constitution. At eighteen, she married her first love, Dr Naidu, under the Special Marriages Act. They had four children in quick succession: Jayasoorya, Padmaja, Leilamani and Ranadheera. Then, at twenty-six, after what seemed like a long apprenticeship, Gosse finally let her publish her first volume of poetry,

---

* As Arthur Symons, in his introduction to *The Golden Threshold*, quotes from her letter:

One day, when I was eleven, I was sighing over a sum in algebra: it wouldn't come right; but instead a whole poem came to me suddenly. I wrote it down.

From that day my 'poetic career' began. At thirteen I wrote a long poem a la 'Lady of the Lake'—1300 lines in six days. At thirteen I wrote a drama of 2000 lines . . . I wrote a novel, I wrote fat volumes of journals. I took myself very seriously in those days.

evocatively titled *The Golden Threshold*. That is what she called her home on Nampally Station Road: a largeish, tree-filled garden house on one of the city's main roads, close to Abid's, the famous department store.

Sarojini, however, chafed against her life of 'sequestered ease'. She longed to play a more important role in national life. Hyderabad, ruled by the Nizams, was a conservative kingdom, with little scope for democratic politics or mass movements, let alone those led by women. Looking to find the right kind of patron, she first tried Romesh Chandra Dutt, an author–translator and Indian Civil Service officer. He encouraged her, but could not bring her spirit to flowering. Then she met Gopal Krishna Gokhale in 1906, who immediately took her under his wing. Already famous for her lilting poetry, Sarojini's stirring oratory soon made her an all-India figure. She came to be known as the 'nightingale of India'.

But the defining moment in her life came when she met Mohandas Karamchand Gandhi in London. Gandhi had already proved himself in South Africa and was almost the Mahatma he came to be known as. On his way back to India, he and his wife found themselves stranded in London because the Great War had broken out. Sarojini was in London too, as was Gokhale. Gandhi returned to India in January 1915. He kept in touch with Sarojini. After the death of Bal Gangadhar Tilak in 1920, Gandhi became the undisputed leader of the Congress and India's freedom struggle led by it. He found in Sarojini a staunch and useful loyalist. In 1925, she succeeded Gandhi as the president of the Congress, the second woman, after Annie Besant, to occupy this high office and the first Indian lady to do so. She remained a poet at heart, but, as she had pledged to Gokhale, her songs were now in the service of the nation.

In retrospect, Sarojini Naidu was clearly the most prominent woman among the leaders of the mass movement who fought for the independence of India. As a nationalist leader, poet, activist for women's rights, orator and celebrity, she was certainly one of the most memorable and colourful Indian women of the first half of the twentieth century. After independence, she became the first woman Governor of any state in independent India when she assumed charge of the United Provinces (later renamed Uttar Pradesh), India's largest and most important state. As one of the principal aides and followers of Mahatma Gandhi, she was often in the limelight and was among the best-known Indian women of her time. She also had an international presence as India's unofficial cultural ambassador and spokesperson of the freedom movement. In her life converge some of the dominant cultural, social and political currents of pre-independence India. Thus, both in her own right and as a representative of her times, Sarojini deserves to be memorialized and studied.*

---

* Some of this material is taken from my edition of *Sarojini Naidu: Selected Poetry and Prose* (New Delhi: HarperCollins, 1993; revised second ed. Rupa & Co., 2010). I received the Homi Bhabha Fellowship (1991–93) for my project on her. When I began my teaching career in India at the University of Hyderabad, the English

Yet, her career exhibited an intriguing paradox. She was one of those great people whose greatness is most difficult to identify and substantiate. Historians of the freedom movement invariably assign to her a minor role in the formation of the Indian nation. Important as a lieutenant and acolyte of Gandhi, by herself and on her own terms, she becomes relatively less so. Certainly, she made no epoch-making original contribution to either the ideology or practice of the struggle against colonialism. Even within the Congress, such an evaluation of her was not uncommon. This was evident even in the manner in which she became the Governor of the United Provinces. It was Dr Bidhan Chandra Roy who was first offered the governorship by Jawaharlal Nehru in July 1947. Roy was in the USA at that time. Sarojini agreed to officiate in his place. When Roy returned to India in November, he decided to accept the more challenging office of the chief minister of West Bengal and consequently resigned his

---

Department operated from the Naidu home, The Golden Threshold. This historic property played host to world-famous leaders, including Mahatma Gandhi, who planted a mango tree on its premises that still survives. Sarojini also grew up in another house nearby. Her father, Dr Aghorenath Chattopadhyay, served the Nizam. His wife, Varadasundari Devi, was a gifted, progressive and extraordinary lady, who was raised in a Brahmo home for girls. They had eight children, all of them quite exceptional, Sarojini being the eldest and Harindranath, the youngest. Other siblings included Mrinalini, or Gunnu Auntie, a renowned educationist who served as principal of Sir Ganga Ram School in Lahore, and Virendranath Chattopadhyaya or Chatto, a prominent revolutionary and Communist leader, who was killed in the Stalinist purges. The family stayed just behind the General Post Office on what is now the Jawaharlal Nehru Road.

governorship. It was only after his resignation that she was 'confirmed' as the Governor of U.P.; otherwise, she was to have handed over the charge by the end of October 1947. Through her entire public life, she never ran for elected office; most likely, she had no grassroots support or base in any part of the country. It is easy, therefore, to see her contribution as merely that of a celebrity publicist and public relations officer of the Congress in general and Gandhi in particular.

Similarly, in the women's movement, Sarojini's contribution was more that of a supporter and popularizer than an original thinker or activist. When one examines the history of the women's movement in India, it was Annie Besant, not Sarojini, who was the pioneer. The prime mover behind the All-India Women's Conference, of which Sarojini was one of the prominent leaders, was Margaret Cousins, another Theosophist and follower of Besant. Sarojini was a non-controversial and famous Indian figurehead who could lend the cause legitimacy and acceptance. Similarly, in the realms of religious ideas or activism, Sarojini was no radical like Pandita Ramabai nor a great organizer like Kamaldevi Chattopadhyaya, who married Sarojini's younger brother, Harindranath, several decades later.

Nowhere is this paradox more obvious than in her poetry. Sarojini's poetry occupies an arguably limited realm of lyricism and is deliberately ephemeral thematically. Her indisputable metrical felicity and technical mastery have not prevented some of her poems from sounding like juvenile jingles. Indeed, with the modernist turn in Indian English poetry in the 1950s, a whole generation of poets grew up despising her poetry. Among them were P. Lal, Nissim Ezekiel, R. Parthasarathy, Adil Jussawalla, A.K. Mehrotra and Keki Daruwalla. Some of them have also been influential anthologists, editors and patrons of Indian English poetry. To them, Sarojini was a particularly soft target: not only did she represent a dead aesthetic, but her romanticism was of a particularly meretricious kind. Whereas Rabindranath Tagore or Sri Aurobindo were harder to demolish or dismiss, Sarojini was a pushover because she had no pretensions to the depth or intellectual range of the other two figures. But, despite her sinking reputation among a whole generation of poets and poet-makers, she has remained one of the most popular, widely-anthologized and studied of Indian English poets. Indeed, there are more books, papers and articles on her poetry than on any Indian poet writing in English, except Sri Aurobindo.

The riddle of the greatness of Sarojini may be solved by realizing that she was a minor figure in a major mode. Whatever she did, on its own terms, may not necessarily have been profound or significant in itself, but it was nevertheless performed on a scale that was extraordinary and central to the formation of the Indian nation. She could sustain this seeming contradiction not only because of the special circumstances in which she lived and which made her qualities rare and sought-after, but because she was truly outstanding in one sphere. Her unusual energy, vitality and verve contributed to an extraordinary public presence, which was both dynamic and catalytic. In other words, her unique greatness lay in aspects of her life and personality that are no longer accessible to us through her written words. The text of Sarojini's greatness was live, not scripted like that of male leaders.

One instance of this lost greatness needs special mention. Sarojini was one of the most eloquent and moving orators of her time, though most of what she spoke had emotional appeal and sentiment rather than 'solid' thought or argumentation. She was not really a great thinker, but a capable one; it was, instead, the force of her personality that created the impact that she was remembered for. She was, perhaps, the most effective purveyor of the sublime, transforming public speaking into poetry. Moreover, Sarojini was an unorthodox and irrepressibly candid person, one who could poke fun at Gandhi himself, not to speak of his more solemn, humourless and puritanical coterie.

Her letters to her children, especially to Padmaja, reveal her as a chatty correspondent, revelling in caricature and witty gossip. As she said to the latter: 'In the course of a long and most variegated life I have learned one superlative truth . . . that the true measure of life and oneself lies not in the circumstances and events that fill its map but in one's approach and attitude and acceptance of those things."* She certainly lived by these words till the end of her days. Finally, her greatness is most evident in her unconventional life. Throughout her eventful and busy years, she overcame extraordinary odds and pushed the realms of activity for Indian women farther than perhaps anyone had done before her.

Thus, while it is easy not to take seriously the adoring and cloying praise of her contemporaries and admirers, it is equally necessary not to swing to the other extreme and dismiss her out of hand. A critical examination of her life and works reveals not only that crucial aspects of her achievement may not be easily accessible to us, but that we need to look afresh at whatever of her life and work is available to us. A career such as Sarojini's not only calls into question how great she really was, but also forces us to re-examine our received notions of 'greatness', which are mostly patriarchal and intellectually elitist.

---

* Padmaja was not only a close associate of Nehru, but served as governor of West Bengal. As one of the founders of the Nehru Memorial Museum and Library, she preserved some of the papers of her mother and also tried to found a similar institution to preserve Sarojini's legacy. It was she who bequeathed The Golden Threshold to the University of Hyderabad and established the Sarojini Naidu Memorial Trust and Museum on the premises of Aghorenath Chattopadhyay's home. That was where I began my acquaintance with Sarojini's fascinating legacy. Apart from working on her poetry, I also edited *Sarojini Naidu: Selected Letters* (New Delhi: Kali for Women, 1992); the quoted letter is from p. 278 of this edition. For me, my engagement with her life and work was nothing short of reclaiming a kinship.

Today, Sarojini's poems are hardly taught or read. Many of the younger generations have barely heard of her and do not have an idea of her remarkable life and contribution to modern India. That is why this edition of *The Essential Sarojini Naidu* is so timely and welcome.

—Makarand R. Paranjape, director,
Indian Institute of Advanced Study, Shimla

A Note on the Selected Writings

Sarojini Naidu wrote prolifically throughout her life. It is her poetry that has been read most widely and that initially propelled her into writing, but she also contributed immensely through her speeches and interactions with people. As a young girl, she became an active part of the freedom struggle and used her mastery over the English language to address people at colleges, functions, protests and gatherings. She also moved resolutions that formally put into words certain demands, such as that for women to be a part of franchise and demand equal rights as men, opposition to the Khilafat movement, and the messages of the Civil Disobedience and Satyagraha movements. Through her writing and speeches, people could identify with these causes, find words that expressed their dissent and unite under one banner to fight for freedom. Though she knew Hindi, Persian and Bengali, a significant part of her writing was in English, the language she was encouraged to learn as a young child by her father.

She would often speak about what she had learnt from Gopal Krishna Gokhale and Mahatma Gandhi, and also use each platform to spread the salient messages of how they wanted people to revolt. Her words were a perfect contribution to the concept of a non-violent freedom struggle. When Gopal Krishna Gokhale passed away, she also wrote an article in his memory in the *Bombay Chronicle*, which has been produced here.

Throughout her life, she also wrote many letters to her family and friends. These provide a glimpse into her personal life and thoughts, and also how she saw her role in the freedom movement and the world.

These writings have been selected to best reflect who she was as a person and the ideals that were most important to her. This is not an exhaustive collection of what she wrote, but the poems, speeches and letters that best encapsulate her style of writing, contributions to the world, the way she saw herself and the way she interacted with the world. Her words made a huge impact not only on the Indians who were fighting to regain control of their country from the British, but also all the other stalwarts she came into contact with, such as Mahatma Gandhi, Jawaharlal Nehru, Rabindranath Tagore and Gopal Krishna Gokhale. Her words live on and continue to inspire, delight and retain her essence.

A Note on the Spellings

The contents of this book have been sourced from archives and other books. All effort has been made to be as accurate as possible, and any errors that may have crept in are limited to this edition and will be corrected in future editions.

The spellings of certain words such as 'Moslem' have been retained in the poems, letters and speeches the way that the author wrote them at her time, and may differ from the way these words are spelt today. This has been done to retain the authenticity of the text and to provide a sense of how Sarojini Naidu would have written or pronounced these words.

POEMS

Introduction to Poems

Sarojini Naidu's poems were read the world over. For the Indians and British in India alike, it was new to see a poet, and especially a woman, write in English and at the same time capture distinctly Indian motifs in her writing. She was taught English at an early age. 'I,' she writes, 'was stubborn and refused to speak it. So one day when I was nine years old my father punished me—the only time I was ever punished—by shutting me in a room alone for a whole day. I came out of it a full-blown linguist. I have never spoken any other language to him, or to my mother, who always speaks to me in Hindustani. I don't think I had any special hankering to write poetry as a little child, though I was of a very fanciful and dreamy nature. My training under my father's eye was of a sternly scientific character. He was determined that I should be a great mathematician or a scientist, but the poetic instinct, which I inherited from him and also from my mother (who wrote some lovely Bengali lyrics in her youth) proved stronger. One day, when I was eleven, I was sighing over a sum in algebra: it WOULDN'T come right; but instead a whole poem came to me suddenly. I wrote it down. From that day my 'poetic career' began. At thirteen I wrote a long poem a la "Lady of the Lake"— 1300 lines in six days. At thirteen I wrote a drama of 2000 lines, a full-fledged passionate thing that I began on the spur of the moment without forethought, just to spite my doctor who said I was very ill and must not touch a book. My health broke down permanently about this time, and my regular studies being stopped I read voraciously. I suppose the greater part of my reading was done between fourteen and sixteen. I wrote a novel, I wrote fat volumes of journals; I took myself very seriously in those days.'

We have her own words to understand how she felt about herself as a poet: 'I don't think I had any special hankering to write poetry as a little child, though I was of a very fanciful and dreamy nature. My training under my father's eye was of a sternly scientific character. He was determined that I should be a great mathematician or a scientist, but the poetic instruct, which I inherited from him and also from my mother (who wrote some lovely Bengali lyrics in her youth), proved stronger. One day, when I was eleven, I was sighing over a sum in Algebra: it wouldn't come right, but instead a whole poem came to me suddenly. I wrote it down. From that day my poetic career began. At thirteen I wrote a long poem a la 'Lady of the Lake'—1,300 lines in six days. At thirteen I wrote a drama of 2,000 lines, a full-fledged passionate thing that I began on the spur of the moment without forethought, just to spite my doctor who said I was very ill and must not touch a book. My health broke down permanently about this time, and my regular studies being stopped I read voraciously.

'I suppose the greater part of my reading was done between fourteen and sixteen. I wrote a novel, I wrote fat volumes of journal. I took myself seriously in those days.'

Sarojini Naidu published three collections of poems during her life—*The Golden Threshold*, *The Bird of Time* and *The Broken Wing*—all of which were first published in the UK. Her large body of work earned her the moniker The Nightingale of India or The Bharat Kokila. The poems in this book have been selected from these three collections, and represent the themes the poet would return to again and again in her writing—love, life, death, spring and pain. A lot of the poems can be sung as songs or narrated along to music.

The Golden Threshold

The Golden Threshold was published in 1905 in London, and the first collection by Sarojini Naidu. She began writing them in 1896, when she was just seventeen and then completed the collection when she was about twenty-five. She decided to dedicate it to Edmund Gosse, writing,

'Who first showed me the way
to the golden threshold'

The entire collection is divided into three parts—Folk Songs, Songs for Music and Poems. This volume contains poems from the Folk Songs and Poems sections. Each of the poems from the first part, i.e., folk songs, is distinctly Indian in setting and elements, whether she is talking about the Indian weavers or drawing inspiration from actual harvest hymns that were sung. This part also contains one of Sarojini Naidu's most famous poems, 'The Palanquin Bearers'. The section titled 'Poems' begins with 'Ode to the Nizam of Hyderabad', which was written for the same Nizam who facilitated her studies at King's College in London.

'The Song of Princess Zeb-un-nissa' is loosely translated from the Persian. She could read and write in Persian fluently. In fact, it was a Persian play she wrote as a twelve-year-old, *Maher Muneer*, that inspired the Nizam to send her to London to study.

The collection contained an introduction by one of her mentors, Arthur Symons. He wrote of the collection: 'It is for this bird-like quality of song, it seems to me, that they are to be valued. They hint, in a sort of delicately evasive way, at a rare temperament, the temperament of a woman of the East, finding expression through a Western language and under partly Western influences.'

When Arthur Symons appreciated the poems Sarojini Naidu had written for the collection, she said, 'Is it possible that I have written verses that are "filled with beauty", and is it possible that you really think them worthy of being given to the world? You know how high my ideal of Art is; and to me my poor casual little poems seem to be less than beautiful—I mean with that final enduring beauty that I desire.' In another letter, she wrote, 'I am not a poet really. I have the vision and the desire, but not the voice. If I could write just one poem full of beauty and the spirit of greatness, I should be exultantly silent for ever; but I sing just as the birds do, and my songs are as ephemeral.'

THE GOLDEN THRESHOLD
FOLK SONGS

Palanquin Bearers

Lightly, O lightly we bear her along,
She sways like a flower in the wind of our song;
She skims like a bird on the foam of a stream,
She floats like a laugh from the lips of a dream.
Gaily, O gaily we glide and we sing,
We bear her along like a pearl on a string.

Softly, O softly we bear her along,
She hangs like a star in the dew of our song;
She springs like a beam on the brow of the tide,
She falls like a tear from the eyes of a bride.
Lightly, O lightly we glide and we sing,
We bear her along like a pearl on a string.

Wandering Singers

(Written to one of their Tunes)

Where the voice of the wind calls our wandering feet,
Through echoing forest and echoing street,
With lutes in our hands ever-singing we roam,
All men are our kindred, the world is our home.

Our lays are of cities whose lustre is shed,
The laughter and beauty of women long dead;
The sword of old battles, the crown of old kings,
And happy and simple and sorrowful things.

What hope shall we gather, what dreams shall we sow?
Where the wind calls our wandering footsteps we go.
No love bids us tarry, no joy bids us wait:
The voice of the wind is the voice of our fate.

Indian Weavers

Weavers, weaving at break of day,
Why do you weave a garment so gay? . . .
Blue as the wing of a halcyon wild,
We weave the robes of a new-born child.

Weavers, weaving at fall of night,
Why do you weave a garment so bright? . . .
Like the plumes of a peacock, purple and green,
We weave the marriage-veils of a queen.

Weavers, weaving solemn and still,
What do you weave in the moonlight chill? . . .
White as a feather and white as a cloud,
We weave a dead man's funeral shroud.

Village-Song

Honey, child, honey, child, whither are you going?
Would you cast your jewels all to the breezes blowing?
Would you leave the mother who on golden grain has
    fed you?
Would you grieve the lover who is riding forth to wed you?

Mother mine, to the wild forest I am going,
Where upon the champa boughs the champa buds are
    blowing;
To the koil-haunted river-isles where lotus lilies glisten,
The voices of the fairy folk are calling me: O listen!

Honey, child, honey, child, the world is full of pleasure,
Of bridal-songs and cradle-songs and sandal-scented
    leisure.
Your bridal robes are in the loom, silver and saffron
    glowing,
Your bridal cakes are on the hearth: O whither are you
    going?

The bridal-songs and cradle-songs have cadences of sorrow,

The laughter of the sun to-day, the wind of death to-
    morrow.
Far sweeter sound the forest-notes where forest-streams
    are falling;
O mother mine, I cannot stay, the fairy-folk are calling.

In Praise of Henna

A kokila called from a henna-spray:
LIRA! LIREE! LIRA! LIREE!
Hasten, maidens, hasten away
To gather the leaves of the henna-tree.
Send your pitchers afloat on the tide,
Gather the leaves ere the dawn be old,
Grind them in mortars of amber and gold,
The fresh green leaves of the henna-tree.

A kokila called from a henna-spray:
LIRA! LIREE! LIRA! LIREE!
Hasten maidens, hasten away
To gather the leaves of the henna-tree.
The tilka's red for the brow of a bride,
And betel-nut's red for lips that are sweet;
But, for lily-like fingers and feet,
The red, the red of the henna-tree.

Harvest Hymn

(men's voices)
Lord of the lotus, lord of the harvest,
Bright and munificent lord of the morn!
Thine is the bounty that prospered our sowing,
Thine is the bounty that nurtured our corn.
We bring thee our songs and our garlands for tribute,
The gold of our fields and the gold of our fruit;
O giver of mellowing radiance, we hail thee,
We praise thee, O Surya, with cymbal and flute.

Lord of the rainbow, lord of the harvest,
Great and beneficent lord of the main!
Thine is the mercy that cherished our furrows,
Thine is the mercy that fostered our grain.
We bring thee our thanks and our garlands for tribute,
The wealth of our valleys, new-garnered and ripe;
O sender of rain and the dewfall, we hail thee,
We praise thee, Varuna, with cymbal and pipe.

(women's voices)
Queen of the gourd-flower, queen of the harvest,

17

Sweet and omnipotent mother, O Earth!
Thine is the plentiful bosom that feeds us,
Thine is the womb where our riches have birth.
We bring thee our love and our garlands for tribute,
With gifts of thy opulent giving we come;
O source of our manifold gladness, we hail thee,
We praise thee, O Prithvi, with cymbal and drum.

(*all voices*)
Lord of the Universe, Lord of our being,
Father eternal, ineffable Om!
Thou art the Seed and the Scythe of our harvests,
Thou art our Hands and our Heart and our Home.
We bring thee our lives and our labours for tribute,
Grant us thy succour, thy counsel, thy care.
O Life of all life and all blessing, we hail thee,
We praise thee, O Bramha, with cymbal and prayer.

Indian Love-Song

(She)
Like a serpent to the calling voice of flutes,
Glides my heart into thy fingers, O my Love!
Where the night-wind, like a lover, leans above
His jasmine-gardens and sirisha-bowers;
And on ripe boughs of many-coloured fruits
Bright parrots cluster like vermilion flowers.

(He)
Like the perfume in the petals of a rose,
Hides thy heart within my bosom, O my love!
Like a garland, like a jewel, like a dove
That hangs its nest in the asoka-tree.
Lie still, O love, until the morning sows
Her tents of gold on fields of ivory.

Cradle-Song

From groves of spice,
O'er fields of rice,
Athwart the lotus-stream,
I bring for you,
Aglint with dew
A little lovely dream.

Sweet, shut your eyes,
The wild fire-flies
Dance through the fairy neem;
From the poppy-bole
For you I stole
A little lovely dream.

Dear eyes, good-night,
In golden light
The stars around you gleam;
On you I press
With soft caress
A little lovely dream.

Suttee

Lamp of my life, the lips of Death
Hath blown thee out with their sudden breath;
Naught shall revive thy vanished spark . . .
Love, must I dwell in the living dark?

Tree of my life, Death's cruel foot
Hath crushed thee down to thy hidden root;
Nought shall restore thy glory fled . . .
Shall the blossom live when the tree is dead?

Life of my life, Death's bitter sword
Hath severed us like a broken word,
Rent us in twain who are but one.
Shall the flesh survive when the soul is gone?

THE GOLDEN THRESHOLD
POEMS

Ode to H.H. The Nizam of Hyderabad

(Presented at the Ramzan Durbar)

Deign, Prince, my tribute to receive,
This lyric offering to your name,
Who round your jewelled scepter bind
The lilies of a poet's fame;
Beneath whose sway concordant dwell
The peoples whom your laws embrace,
In brotherhood of diverse creeds,
And harmony of diverse race:

The votaries of the Prophet's faith,
Of whom you are the crown and chief
And they, who bear on Vedic brows
Their mystic symbols of belief;

And they, who worshipping the sun,
Fled o'er the old Iranian sea;
And they, who bow to Him who trod
The midnight waves of Galilee.

Sweet, sumptuous fables of Baghdad
The splendours of your court recall,
The torches of a Thousand Nights
Blaze through a single festival;
And Saki-singers down the streets,
Pour for us, in a stream divine,
From goblets of your love-ghazals
The rapture of your Sufi wine.

Prince, where your radiant cities smile,
Grim hills their sombre vigils keep,
Your ancient forests hoard and hold
The legends of their centuried sleep;
Your birds of peace white-pinioned float
O'er ruined fort and storied plain,
Your faithful stewards sleepless guard
The harvests of your gold and grain.

God give you joy, God give you grace
To shield the truth and smite the wrong,
To honour Virtue, Valour, Worth.
To cherish faith and foster song.
So may the lustre of your days
Outshine the deeds Firdusi sung,
Your name within a nation's prayer,
Your music on a nation's tongue.

Past and Future

The new hath come and now the old retires:
And so the past becomes a mountain-cell,
Where lone, apart, old hermit-memories dwell
In consecrated calm, forgotten yet
Of the keen heart that hastens to forget
Old longings in fulfilling new desires.

And now the Soul stands in a vague, intense
Expectancy and anguish of suspense,
On the dim chamber-threshold . . . lo! he sees
Like a strange, fated bride as yet unknown,
His timid future shrinking there alone,
Beneath her marriage-veil of mysteries.

Life

Children, ye have not lived, to you it seems
Life is a lovely stalactite of dreams,
Or carnival of careless joys that leap
About your hearts like billows on the deep
In flames of amber and of amethyst.

Children, ye have not lived, ye but exist
Till some resistless hour shall rise and move
Your hearts to wake and hunger after love,
And thirst with passionate longing for the things
That burn your brows with blood-red sufferings.

Till ye have battled with great grief and fears,
And borne the conflict of dream-shattering years,
Wounded with fierce desire and worn with strife,
Children, ye have not lived: for this is life.

The Poet's Love-Song

In noon-tide hours, O Love, secure and strong,
I need thee not; mad dreams are mine to bind
The world to my desire, and hold the wind
A voiceless captive to my conquering song.
I need thee not, I am content with these:
Keep silence in thy soul, beyond the seas!

But in the desolate hour of midnight, when
An ecstasy of starry silence sleeps
On the still mountains and the soundless deeps,
And my soul hungers for thy voice, O then,
Love, like the magic of wild melodies,
Let thy soul answer mine across the seas.

To the God of Pain

Unwilling priestess in thy cruel fane,
Long hast thou held me, pitiless god of Pain,
Bound to thy worship by reluctant vows,
My tired breast girt with suffering, and my brows
Anointed with perpetual weariness.
Long have I borne thy service, through the stress
Of rigorous years, sad days and slumberless nights,
Performing thine inexorable rites.

For thy dark altars, balm nor milk nor rice,
But mine own soul thou'st ta'en for sacrifice:
All the rich honey of my youth's desire,
And all the sweet oils from my crushed life drawn,
And all my flower-like dreams and gem-like fire
Of hopes up-leaping like the light of dawn.

I have no more to give, all that was mine
Is laid, a wrested tribute, at thy shrine;
Let me depart, for my whole soul is wrung,
And all my cheerless orisons are sung;
Let me depart, with faint limbs let me creep
To some dim shade and sink me down to sleep.

The Song of Princess Zeb-Un-Nissa
In Praise of Her Own Beauty

(From the Persian)

When from my cheek I lift my veil,
The roses turn with envy pale,
And from their pierced hearts, rich with pain,
Send forth their fragrance like a wail.

Or if perchance one perfumed tress
Be lowered to the wind's caress,
The honeyed hyacinths complain,
And languish in a sweet distress.

And, when I pause, still groves among,
(Such loveliness is mine) a throng
Of nightingales awake and strain
Their souls into a quivering song.

Indian Dancers

Eyes ravished with rapture, celestially panting,
what passionate bosoms aflaming with fire
Drink deep of the hush of the hyacinth
heavens that glimmer around them in
fountains of light;
O wild and entrancing the strain of keen music
that cleaveth the stars like a wail of desire,
And beautiful dancers with houri-like faces
bewitch the voluptuous watches of night.

The scents of red roses and sandalwood flutter
and die in the maze of their gem-tangled hair,
And smiles are entwining like magical serpents
the poppies of lips that are opiate-sweet;
Their glittering garments of purple are burning
like tremulous dawns in the quivering air,
And exquisite, subtle and slow are the tinkle
and tread of their rhythmical, slumber-soft feet.

Now silent, now singing and swaying and swinging,
like blossoms that bend to the breezes or showers,

Now wantonly winding, they flash, now they
falter, and, lingering, languish in radiant
choir;
Their jewel-girt arms and warm, wavering, lily-long
fingers enchant through melodious hours,
Eyes ravished with rapture, celestially panting,
what passionate bosoms aflaming with fire!

The Queen's Rival

Queen Gulnaar sat on her ivory bed,
Around her countless treasures were spread;

Her chamber walls were richly inlaid
With agate, porphory, onyx and jade;

The tissues that veiled her delicate breast,
Glowed with the hues of a lapwing's crest;

But still she gazed in her mirror and sighed
'O King, my heart is unsatisfied.'

King Feroz bent from his ebony seat:
'Is thy least desire unfulfilled, O Sweet?

'Let thy mouth speak and my life be spent
To clear the sky of thy discontent.'

'I tire of my beauty, I tire of this
Empty splendour and shadowless bliss;

'With none to envy and none gainsay,
No savour or salt hath my dream or day.'

Queen Gulnaar sighed like a murmuring rose:
'Give me a rival, O King Feroz.'

II

King Feroz spoke to his Chief Vizier:
'Lo! ere to-morrow's dawn be here,

'Send forth my messengers over the sea,
To seek seven beautiful brides for me;

'Radiant of feature and regal of mien,
Seven handmaids meet for the Persian Queen.' . . .

Seven new moon tides at the Vesper call,
King Feroz led to Queen Gulnaar's hall

A young queen eyed like the morning star:
'I bring thee a rival, O Queen Gulnaar.'

But still she gazed in her mirror and sighed:
'O King, my heart is unsatisfied.'

Seven queens shone round her ivory bed,
Like seven soft gems on a silken thread,

Like seven fair lamps in a royal tower,
Like seven bright petals of Beauty's flower

Queen Gulnaar sighed like a murmuring rose
'Where is my rival, O King Feroz?'

III

When spring winds wakened the mountain floods,
And kindled the flame of the tulip buds,

When bees grew loud and the days grew long,
And the peach groves thrilled to the oriole's song,

Queen Gulnaar sat on her ivory bed,
Decking with jewels her exquisite head;

And still she gazed in her mirror and sighed:
'O King, my heart is unsatisfied.'

Queen Gulnaar's daughter two spring times old,
In blue robes bordered with tassels of gold,

Ran to her knee like a wildwood fay,
And plucked from her hand the mirror away.

Quickly she set on her own light curls
Her mother's fillet with fringes of pearls;

Quickly she turned with a child's caprice
And pressed on the mirror a swift, glad kiss.

Queen Gulnaar laughed like a tremulous rose:
'Here is my rival, O King Feroz.'

The Poet to Death

Tarry a while, O Death, I cannot die
While yet my sweet life burgeons with its spring;
Fair is my youth, and rich the echoing boughs
Where dhadikulas sing.

Tarry a while, O Death, I cannot die
With all my blossoming hopes unharvested,
My joys ungarnered, all my songs unsung,
And all my tears unshed.

Tarry a while, till I am satisfied
Of love and grief, of earth and altering sky;
Till all my human hungers are fulfilled,
O Death, I cannot die!

The Pardah Nashin

Her life is a revolving dream
Of languid and sequestered ease;
Her girdles and her fillets gleam
Like changing fires on sunset seas;
Her raiment is like morning mist,
Shot opal, gold and amethyst.

From thieving light of eyes impure,
From coveting sun or wind's caress,
Her days are guarded and secure
Behind her carven lattices,
Like jewels in a turbaned crest,
Like secrets in a lover's breast.

But though no hand unsanctioned dares
Unveil the mysteries of her grace,
Time lifts the curtain unawares,
And Sorrow looks into her face . . .
Who shall prevent the subtle years,
Or shield a woman's eyes from tears?

To Youth

O Youth, sweet comrade Youth, wouldst thou be gone?
Long have we dwelt together, thou and I;
Together drunk of many an alien dawn,
And plucked the fruit of many an alien sky.

Ah, fickle friend, must I, who yesterday
Dreamed forwards to long, undimmed ecstasy,
Henceforward dream, because thou wilt not stay,
Backward to transient pleasure and to thee?

I give thee back thy false, ephemeral vow;
But, O beloved comrade, ere we part,
Upon my mournful eyelids and my brow
Kiss me who hold thine image in my heart.

Nightfall in the City of Hyderabad

See how the speckled sky burns like a pigeon's throat,
Jewelled with embers of opal and peridot.

See the white river that flashes and scintillates,
Curved like a tusk from the mouth of the city-gates.

Hark, from the minaret, how the muezzin's call
Floats like a battle-flag over the city wall.

From trellised balconies, languid and luminous
Faces gleam, veiled in a splendour voluminous.

Leisurely elephants wind through the winding lanes,
Swinging their silver bells hung from their silver chains.

Round the high Char Minar sounds of gay cavalcades
Blend with the music of cymbals and serenades.

Over the city bridge Night comes majestical,
Borne like a queen to a sumptuous festival.

Street Cries

When dawn's first cymbals beat upon the sky,
Rousing the world to labour's various cry,
To tend the flock, to bind the mellowing grain,
From ardent toil to forge a little gain,
And fasting men go forth on hurrying feet,
BUY BREAD, BUY BREAD, rings down the eager street.

When the earth falters and the waters swoon
With the implacable radiance of noon,
And in dim shelters koils hush their notes,
And the faint, thirsting blood in languid throats
Craves liquid succour from the cruel heat,
BUY FRUIT, BUY FRUIT, steals down the panting street.

When twilight twinkling o'er the gay bazaars,
Unfurls a sudden canopy of stars,
When lutes are strung and fragrant torches lit
On white roof-terraces where lovers sit
Drinking together of life's poignant sweet,
BUY FLOWERS, BUY FLOWERS, floats down the
    singing street.

To India

O young through all thy immemorial years!
Rise, Mother, rise, regenerate from thy gloom,
And, like a bride high-mated with the spheres,
Beget new glories from thine ageless womb!

The nations that in fettered darkness weep
Crave thee to lead them where great mornings break . . .
Mother, O Mother, wherefore dost thou sleep?
Arise and answer for thy children's sake!

Thy Future calls thee with a manifold sound
To crescent honours, splendours, victories vast;
Waken, O slumbering Mother and be crowned,
Who once wert empress of the sovereign Past.

The Royal Tombs of Golconda

I muse among these silent fanes
Whose spacious darkness guards your dust;
Around me sleep the hoary plains
That hold your ancient wars in trust.
I pause, my dreaming spirit hears,
Across the wind's unquiet tides,
The glimmering music of your spears,
The laughter of your royal brides.

In vain, O Kings, doth time aspire
To make your names oblivion's sport,
While yonder hill wears like a tier
The ruined grandeur of your fort.
Though centuries falter and decline,
Your proven strongholds shall remain
Embodied memories of your line,
Incarnate legends of your reign.

O Queens, in vain old Fate decreed
Your flower-like bodies to the tomb;
Death is in truth the vital seed

Of your imperishable bloom
Each new-born year the bulbuls sing
Their songs of your renascent loves;
Your beauty wakens with the spring
To kindle these pomegranate groves.

The Bird of Time

The Bird of Time was the second collection, published seven years later in 1912. It contains one of her most popular poems, 'In the Bazaars of Hyderabad'. It contains an introduction by Edmund Gosse, who the first collection was dedicated to. Of her and her writing, he said, 'Mrs. Naidu is, I believe, acknowledged to be the most accomplished living poet of India—at least, of those who write in English . . . In a gracious sentence, published seven or eight years ago, Sarojini Naidu declared that it was the writer of this preface "who first showed" her "the way to the golden threshold" of poetry. This is her generous mode of describing certain conditions which I may perhaps be allowed to enlarge upon so far as they throw light on the contents of the volume before us.

It is needless for me to repeat those particulars of the Indian poet's early life, so picturesque and so remarkable, which were given by Mr. Arthur Symons in the excellent essay which he prefixed to her volume of 1905. Sufficient for my purpose it is to say that when Sarojini Chattopddhyay—as she then was—first made her appearance in London, she was a child of sixteen years, but as unlike the usual English maiden of that age as a lotus or a cactus is unlike a lily of the valley. She was already marvellous in mental maturity, amazingly well read, and far beyond a Western child in all her acquaintance with the world.

'I implored her to consider that from a young Indian of extreme sensibility, who had mastered not merely the language but the prosody of the West, what we wished to receive was, not a réchauffé of Anglo-Saxon sentiment in an Anglo-Saxon setting, but some revelation of the heart of India. Moreover, I entreated Sarojini to write no more about robins and skylarks, in a landscape of our Midland counties, with the village bells somewhere in the distance calling the parishioners to church, but to describe the flowers, the fruits, the trees, to set her poems firmly among the mountains, the gardens, the temples, to introduce to us the vivid populations of her own voluptuous and unfamiliar province; in other words, to be a genuine Indian poet of the Deccan.'

Sarojini Naidu wrote to Edmund Gosse to say, 'While I live, it will always be the supreme desire of my Soul to write poetry—one poem, one line of enduring verse even. Perhaps I shall die without realising that longing which is at once an exquisite joy and an unspeakable anguish to me.'

The poems in this collection are no longer from the lens of a young girl, an indication of the time she had spent in India since returning from Britain and joining the freedom struggle. The poems are definitely more patriotic and imbued with love for her country. They also reflect a lot more of the themes of life, death and pain, which would come to occupy her for the rest of her life and writing.

The Bird of Time

O Bird of Time on your fruitful bough
What are the songs you sing? . . .
Songs of the glory and gladness of life,
Of poignant sorrow and passionate strife,
And the lilting joy of the spring;
Of hope that sows for the years unborn,
And faith that dreams of a tarrying morn,
The fragrant peace of the twilight's breath,
And the mystic silence that men call death.

O Bird of Time, say where did you learn
The changing measures you sing? . . .
In blowing forests and breaking tides,
In the happy laughter of new-made brides,
And the nests of the new-born spring;
In the dawn that thrills to a mother's prayer,
And the night that shelters a heart's despair,
In the sigh of pity, the sob of hate,
And the pride of a soul that has conquered fate

Love and Death

I dreamed my love had set thy spirit free,
Enfranchised thee from Fate's o'ermastering power,
And girt thy being with a scatheless dower
Of rich and joyous immortality;
O Love, I dreamed my soul had ransomed thee,
In thy lone, dread, incalculable hour
From those pale hands at which all mortals cower,
And conquered Death by Love, like Savitri.
When I awoke, alas, my love was vain
E'en to annul one throe of destined pain,
Or by one heart-beat to prolong thy breath;
O Love, alas, that love could not assuage
The burden of thy human heritage,
Or save thee from the swift decrees of Death.

A Love Song from the North

Tell me no more of thy love, *papeeha*,
Wouldst thou recall to my heart, *papeeha*,
Dreams of delight that are gone,
When swift to my side came the feet of my lover
With stars of the dusk and the dawn?
I see the soft wings of the clouds on the river,
And jewelled with raindrops the mango-leaves quiver,
And tender boughs flower on the plain. . . .
But what is their beauty to me, *papeeha*,
Beauty of blossom and shower, *papeeha*,
That brings not my lover again?

Tell me no more of thy love, *papeeha*,
Wouldst thou revive in my heart, *papeeha*,
Grief for the joy that is gone?
I hear the bright peacock in glimmering woodlands
Cry to its mate in the dawn;
I hear the black *koel's* slow, tremulous wooing,
And sweet in the gardens the calling and cooing

Of passionate bulbul and dove. . . .
But what is their music to me, *papeeha*,
Songs of their laughter and love, *papeeha*,
To me, forsaken of love?

Alone

Alone, O Love, I seek the blossoming glades,
The bright, accustomed alleys of delight,
Pomegranate-gardens of the mellowing dawn,
Serene and sumptuous orchards of the night.

Alone, O Love, I breast the shimmering waves,
The changing tides of life's familiar streams,
Wide seas of hope, swift rivers of desire,
The moon-enchanted estuary of dreams.

But no compassionate wind or comforting star
Brings me sweet word of thine abiding place . . .
In what predestined hour of joy or tears
Shall I attain the sanctuary of thy face?

A Persian Love Song

O Love! I know not why, when you are glad,
Gaily my glad heart leaps.
Love! I know not why, when you are sad,
Wildly my sad heart weeps.

I know not why, if sweet be your repose,
My waking heart finds rest,
Or if your eyes be dim with pain, sharp throes
Of anguish rend my breast.

Hourly this subtle mystery flowers anew,
O Love, I know not why . . .
Unless it be, perchance, that I am you,
Dear love, that you are I!

Vasant Panchami

Lilavati's Lament at the Feast of Spring

Go, dragon-fly, fold up your purple wing,
Why will you bring me tidings of the spring?
O lilting *koels*, hush your rapturous notes,
O *dhadikulas*, still your passionate throats,
Or seek some further garden for your nest . . .
Your songs are poisoned arrows in my breast.

O quench your flame, ye crimson *gulmohors*,
That flaunt your dazzling bloom across my doors,
Furl your white bells, sweet *champa* buds that call
Wild bees to your ambrosial festival,
And hold your breath, O dear *sirisha* trees . . .
You slay my heart with bitter memories.

O joyous girls who rise at break of morn
With sandal-soil your thresholds to adorn,
Ye brides who streamward bear on jewelled feet
Your gifts of silver lamps and new-blown wheat,

I pray you dim your voices when you sing
Your radiant salutations to the spring.

Hai! what have I to do with nesting birds,
With lotus-honey, corn and ivory curds,
With plantain blossom and pomegranate fruit,
Or rose-wreathed lintels and rose-scented lute,
With lighted shrines and fragrant altar-fires
Where happy women breathe their hearts' desires?

For my sad life is doomed to be, alas,
Ruined and sere like sorrow-trodden grass,
My heart hath grown, plucked by the wind of grief,
Akin to fallen flower and faded leaf,
Akin to every lone and withered thing
That hath foregone the kisses of the spring.

In Praise of Gulmohur Blossoms

What can rival your lovely hue
O gorgeous boon of the spring?
The glimmering red of a bridal robe,
Rich red of a wild bird's wing?
Or the mystic blaze of the gem that burns
On the brow of a serpent-king?

What can rival the valiant joy
Of your dazzling, fugitive sheen?
The limpid clouds of the lustrous dawn
That colour the ocean's mien?
Or the blood that poured from a thousand breasts
To succour a Rajput queen?

What can rival the radiant pride
Of your frail, victorious fire?
The flame of hope or the flame of hate,
Quick flame of my heart's desire?
Or the rapturous light that leaps to heaven
From a true wife's funeral pyre?

Champak Blossoms

Amber petals, ivory petals,
Petals of carven jade,
Charming with your ambrosial sweetness
Forest and field and glade,
Foredoomed in your hour of transient glory
To shrivel and shrink and fade!

Tho' mango blossoms have long since vanished,
And orange blossoms be shed,
They live anew in the luscious harvests
Of ripening yellow and red;
But you, when your delicate bloom is over,
Will reckon amongst the dead.

Only to girdle a girl's dark tresses
Your fragrant hearts are uncurled:
Only to garland the vernal breezes
Your fragile stars are unfurled.
You make no boast in your purposeless beauty
To serve or profit the world.

Yet, 'tis of you thro' the moonlit ages
That maidens and minstrels sing,
And lay your buds on the great god's altar,
O radiant blossoms that fling
Your rich, voluptuous, magical perfume
To ravish the winds of spring.

Slumber Song for Sunalini

In a Bengalee Metre

Where the golden, glowing
Champak-buds are blowing,
By the swiftly-flowing streams,
Now, when day is dying,
There are fairies flying
Scattering a cloud of dreams.

Slumber-spirits winging
Thro' the forest singing,
Flutter hither bringing soon,
Baby-visions sheeny
For my Sunalini . . .
Hush thee, O my pretty moon!

Sweet, the saints shall bless thee . . .
Hush, mine arms caress thee,
Hush, my heart doth press thee, sleep,
Till the red dawn dances
Breaking thy soft trances,
Sleep, my Sunalini, sleep!

Songs of My City

I. In a Latticed Balcony

How shall I feed thee, Beloved?
On golden-red honey and fruit.
How shall I please thee, Beloved?
With th' voice of the cymbal and lute.

How shall I garland thy tresses?
With pearls from the jessamine close.
How shall I perfume thy fingers?
With th' soul of the keora and rose.

How shall I deck thee, O Dearest?
In hues of the peacock and dove.
How shall I woo thee, O Dearest?
With the delicate silence of love.

II. In the Bazaars of Hyderabad

To a Tune of the Bazaars

What do you sell, O ye merchants?
Richly your wares are displayed.
Turbans of crimson and silver,
Tunics of purple brocade,
Mirrors with panels of amber,
Daggers with handles of jade.

What do you weigh, O ye vendors?
Saffron and lentil and rice.
What do you grind, O ye maidens?
Sandalwood, henna, and spice.
What do you call, O ye pedlars?
Chessmen and ivory dice.

What do you make, O ye goldsmiths?
Wristlet and anklet and ring,
Bells for the feet of blue pigeons,
Frail as a dragon-fly's wing,
Girdles of gold for the dancers,

Scabbards of gold for the king.

What do you cry, O ye fruitmen?
Citron, pomegranate, and plum.
What do you play, O musicians?
Cithār, sarangī, and drum.
What do you chant, O magicians?
Spells for the æons to come.

What do you weave, O ye flower-girls
With tassels of azure and red?
Crowns for the brow of a bridegroom,
Chaplets to garland his bed,
Sheets of white blossoms new-gathered
To perfume the sleep of the dead.

Bangle-Sellers

Bangle-sellers are we who bear
Our shining loads to the temple fair. . . .
Who will buy these delicate, bright
Rainbow-tinted circles of light?
Lustrous tokens of radiant lives,
For happy daughters and happy wives.

Some are meet for a maiden's wrist,
Silver and blue as the mountain-mist,
Some are flushed like the buds that dream
On the tranquil brow of a woodland stream;
Some are aglow with the bloom that cleaves
To the limpid glory of new-born leaves.

Some are like fields of sunlit corn,
Meet for a bride on her bridal morn,
Some, like the flame of her marriage fire,
Or rich with the hue of her heart's desire,
Tinkling, luminous, tender, and clear,
Like her bridal laughter and bridal tear.

Some are purple and gold-flecked grey,
For her who has journeyed thro' life midway,
Whose hands have cherished, whose love has blest
And cradled fair sons on her faithful breast,
Who serves her household in fruitful pride,
And worships the gods at her husband's side.

Song of Radha the Milkmaid

I carried my curds to the Mathura fair.....
How softly the heifers were lowing. ....
I wanted to cry 'Who will buy, who will buy
These curds that are white as the clouds in the sky
When the breezes of *Shrawan* are blowing?'
But my heart was so full of your beauty, Beloved,
They laughed as I cried without knowing:
Govinda! Govinda!
Govinda! Govinda! ...
How softly the river was flowing!

I carried my pots to the Mathura tide....
How gaily the rowers were rowing! ...
My comrades called 'Ho! let us dance, let us sing
And wear saffron garments to welcome the spring,
And pluck the new buds that are blowing.'
But my heart was so full of your music, Beloved,
They mocked when I cried without knowing:
Govinda! Govinda!
Govinda! Govinda! ...
How gaily the river was flowing!

I carried my gifts to the Mathura shrine. . . .
How brightly the torches were glowing! . . .
I folded my hands at the altars to pray
'O shining Ones guard us by night and by day'—
And loudly the conch shells were blowing.
But my heart was so lost in your worship, Beloved,
They were wroth when I cried without knowing:
Govinda! Govinda!
Govinda! Govinda! . . .
How brightly the river was flowing!

Hymn to Indra, Lord of Rain

Men's Voices:
O Thou, who rousest the voice of the thunder,
And biddest the storms to awake from their sleep,
Who breakest the strength of the mountains asunder,
And cleavest the manifold pride of the deep!
Thou, who with bountiful torrent and river
Dost nourish the heart of the forest and plain,
Withhold not Thy gifts O Omnipotent Giver!
Hearken, O Lord of Rain!

Women's Voices:
O Thou, who wieldest Thy deathless dominion
O'er mutable legions of earth and the sky,
Who grantest the eagle the joy of her pinion,
And teachest the young of the *koel* to fly!
Thou who art mighty to succour and cherish,
Who savest from sorrow and shieldest from pain,
Withhold not Thy merciful love, or we perish,
Hearken, O Lord of Rain!

Death and Life

Death stroked my hair and whispered tenderly:
'Poor child, shall I redeem thee from thy pain,
Renew thy joy and issue thee again
Inclosed in some renascent ecstasy . . .
Some lilting bird or lotus-loving bee,
Or the diaphanous silver of the rain,
Th' alluring scent of the sirisha-plain,
The wild wind's voice, the white wave's melody?'

I said, 'Thy gentle pity shames mine ear,
O Death, am I so purposeless a thing,
Shall my soul falter or my body fear
Its poignant hour of bitter suffering,
Or fail ere I achieve my destined deed
Of song or service for my country's need?'

The Hussain Saagar

The young dawn woos thee with his amorous grace,
The journeying clouds of sunset pause and hover,
Drinking the beauty of thy luminous face,
But none thine inmost glory may discover,
For thine evasive silver doth enclose
What secret purple and what subtle rose
Responsive only to the wind, thy lover.
Only for him thy shining waves unfold
Translucent music answering his control;
Thou dost, like me, to one allegiance hold,
O lake, O living image of my soul.

The Soul's Prayer

In childhood's pride I said to Thee:
'O Thou, who mad'st me of Thy breath,
Speak, Master, and reveal to me
Thine inmost laws of life and death.

'Give me to drink each joy and pain
Which Thine eternal hand can mete,
For my insatiate soul would drain
Earth's utmost bitter, utmost sweet.

'Spare me no bliss, no pang of strife,
Withhold no gift or grief I crave,
The intricate lore of love and life
And mystic knowledge of the grave.'

Lord, Thou didst answer stern and low:
'Child, I will hearken to thy prayer,
And thy unconquered soul shall know
All passionate rapture and despair.

'Thou shalt drink deep of joy and fame,
And love shall burn thee like a fire,
And pain shall cleanse thee like a flame,
To purge the dross from thy desire.

'So shall thy chastened spirit yearn
To seek from its blind prayer release,
And spent and pardoned, sue to learn
The simple secret of My peace.

'I, bending from my sevenfold height
Will teach thee of My quickening grace,
Life is a prism of My light,
And Death the shadow of My face.'

The Old Woman

A lonely old woman sits out in the street
'Neath the boughs of a banyan tree,
And hears the bright echo of hurrying feet,
The pageant of life going blithely and fleet
To the feast of eternity.

Her tremulous hand holds a battered white bowl,
If perchance in your pity you fling her a dole;
She is poor, she is bent, she is blind,
But she lifts a brave heart to the jest of the days,
And her withered, brave voice croons its paean of praise,
Be the gay world kind or unkind:
'*La ilaha illa-l-Allah,*
La ilaha illa-l-Allah,
Muhammad-ar-Rasul-Allah.'
In hope of your succour, how often in vain,
So patient she sits at my gates,
In the face of the sun and the wind and the rain,
Holding converse with poverty, hunger and pain,
And the ultimate sleep that awaits. . . .
In her youth she hath comforted lover and son,

In her weary old age. O dear God, is there none
To bless her tired eyelids to rest? . . .
Tho' the world may not tarry to help her or heed,
More clear than the cry of her sorrow and need
Is the faith that doth solace her breast:
'*La ilaha illa-l-Allah,*
La ilaha illa-l-Allah,
Muhammad-ar-Rasul-Allah.'

In Salutation to the Eternal Peace

Men say the world is full of fear and hate,
And all life's ripening harvest-fields await
The restless sickle of relentless fate.

But I, sweet Soul, rejoice that I was born,
When from the climbing terraces of corn
I watch the golden orioles of Thy morn.

What care I for the world's desire and pride,
Who know the silver wings that gleam and glide,
The homing pigeons of Thine eventide?

What care I for the world's loud weariness,
Who dream in twilight granaries Thou dost bless
With delicate sheaves of mellow silences?
Say, shall I heed dull presages of doom,
Or dread the rumoured loneliness and gloom,
The mute and mythic terror of the tomb?

For my glad heart is drunk and drenched with Thee,
O inmost wine of living ecstasy!
O intimate essence of eternity!

The Broken Wing

Sarojini Naidu's third collection of poems, *The Broken Wing*, was published in 1917, five years after her second collection. It was published after the death of Gopal Krishna Gokhale in 1915, and the impact that his passing had on her is clear in the titular poem, which opens from a lines he had said to her in one of their correspondences 'Why should a song-bird like you have a broken wing?'. Sarojini Naidu had suffered from illness most of her life and as she grew older, her ailments would often see her confined to bed. Her condition is what had prompted him to say these words to her.

Her feelings about life and the pain it brings are more apparent in the poems she wrote as part of the collection. It contains one of her famous poems, *The Gift of India*, which charts an evolution of her feelings towards the freedom struggle, with her ideals and the demands of the struggle clearer at this stage in her life.

The Broken Wing

'Why should a song-bird like
you have a broken wing?'

G.K. Gokhale

Question

The great dawn breaks, the mournful night is past,
From her deep age-long sleep she wakes at last!
Sweet and long-slumbering buds of gladness ope
Fresh lips to the returning winds of hope.
Our eager hearts renew their radiant flight
Towards the glory of renascent light,
Life and our land await their destined spring . . .
Song-bird why dost you bear a broken wing?

Answer

Shall spring that wakes mine ancient land again
Call to my wild and suffering heart in vain?
Or Fate's blind arrows still the pulsing note
Of my far-reaching, frail, unconquered throat?

Or a weak bleeding pinion daunt or tire
My flight to the high realms of my desire?
Behold! I rise to meet the destined spring
And scale the stars upon my broken wing!

The Gift of India

Is there aught you need that my hands withhold,
Rich gifts of raiment or grain or gold?
Lo! I have flung to the East and West
Priceless treasures torn from my breast.
And yielded the sons of my stricken womb
To the drum-beats of duty, the sabres of doom.

Gathered like pearls in their alien graves
Silent they sleep by the Persian waves,
Scattered like shells on Egyptian sands.
They lie with pale brows and brave, broken hands.
They are strewn like blossoms mown down by chance
On the blood-brown meadows of Flanders and France.

Can ye measure the grief of the tears I weep
Or compass the woe of the watch I keep?

Or the pride that thrills thro' my heart's despair.
And the hope that comforts the anguish of prayer?
And the far sad glorious vision I see
Of the torn red banners of Victory?

When the terror and tumult of hate shall cease
And life be refashioned on anvils of peace,
And your love shall offer memorial thanks
To the comrades who fought in your dauntless ranks.
And you honour the deeds of the deathless ones
Remember the blood of thy martyred sons!

August 1915

The Imam Bara

I

Out of the sombre shadows,
Over the sunlit grass,
Slow in a sad procession
The shadowy pageants pass
Mournful, majestic, and solemn.
Stricken and pale and dumb,
Crowned in their peerless anguish
The sacred martyrs come.
Hark, from the brooding silence
Breaks the wild cry of pain
Wrung from the heart of the ages
Ali! Hassan! Hussain!

Of Lucknow
II

Come from this tomb of shadows,
Come from this tragic shrine

That throbs with the deathless sorrow
Of a long-dead martyr line.
Love! let the living sunlight
Kindle your splendid eyes
Ablaze with the steadfast triumph
Of the spirit that never dies.
So may the hope of new ages
Comfort the mystic pain
That cries from the ancient silence
AH! Hassan! Hussain!

*The Imam Bara is a Chapel of Lamentation
where Mussulmans of the Shiah Community
celebrate the tragic martyrdom of AH, Hassan,
and Hussain during the mourning month of
Moharram. A sort of passion-play takes
place to the accompaniment of the refrain,
Ali! Hassan! Hussain!*

Imperial Delhi

Imperial City! dowered with sovereign grace
To thy renascent glory still there clings
The splendid tragedy of ancient things,
The regal woes of many a vanquished race;
And memory's tears are cold upon thy face
E'en while thy heart's returning gladness rings
Loud on the sleep of thy forgotten kings,
Who in thine arms sought Life's last resting-place.

Thy changing kings and kingdoms pass away
The gorgeous legends of a bygone day,
But thou dost still immutably remain
Unbroken symbol of proud histories,
Unageing priestess of old mysteries
Before whose shrine the spells of Death are vain.

1912

Gokhale*

Heroic Heart! lost hope of all our days!
Need'st thou the homage of our love or praise?
Lo! let the mournful millions round thy pyre
Kindle their souls with consecrated fire
Caught from the brave torch fallen from thy hand.
To succour and to serve our suffering land
And in a daily worship taught by thee
Upbuild the temple of her Unity.

February 19, 1915

* Gopal Krishna Gokhale, the great saint and
soldier of our national righteousness. His
life was a sacrament, and his death was a
sacrifice in the cause of Indian unity.

In Salutation to My Father's Spirit

Aghorenath Chattopadhyay

Farewell, farewell, O brave and tender Sage.
O mystic jester, golden-hearted Child!
Selfless, serene, untroubled, unbeguiled
By trivial snares of grief and greed or rage;
O splendid dreamer in a dreamless age
Whose deep alchemic vision reconciled
Time's changing message with the undefiled
Calm wisdom of thy Vedic heritage!

Farewell great spirit, without rear or flaw.
Thy life was love and liberty thy law.
And Truth thy pure imperishable goal . . .
All hail to thee in thy transcendent flight
From hope to hope, from height to heav'nlier height.
Lost in the rapture of the Cosmic Soul.

January 28, 1915

Farewell

Farewell, O eager faces that surround me.
Claiming the tender service of my days.
Farewell, O joyous spirits that have bound me
With the love-sprinkled garlands of your praise!

O golden lamps of hope how shall I bring you
Life's kindling flame from a forsaken fire?
O glowing hearts of youth, how shall I sing you
Life's glorious message from a broken lyre?

To you what further homage shall I render,
Victorious City girdled by the sea.
Where breaks in surging tides of woe and splendour
The age-long tumult of Humanity?

Need you another tribute ror a token
Who reft from me the pride of all my years?
Lo! I will leave you with farewell unspoken,
Shrine of dead dream! O temple of my tears!

The Call of Spring

To Padmaja and Lilamani

Children, my children, the spring wakes anew.
And calls through the dawn and the daytime
For flower-like and fleet-footed maidens like you.
To share in the joy of its playtime.

O'er hill-side and valley, through garden and grove.
Such exquisite anthems are ringing
Where rapturous bulbul and maina and dove
Their carols of welcome are singing.

I know where the ivory lilies unfold
In brooklets half-hidden in sedges.
And the air is aglow with the blossoming gold
Of thickets and hollows and hedges.

I know where the dragon-flies glimmer and glide,
And the plumes of wild peacocks are gleaming.
Where the fox and the squirrel and timid fawn hide
And the hawk and the heron Ue dreaming.

The earth is ashine like a hummmg-bird's wmg,
And the sky like a kingfisher's feather,
O come, let us go and play with the spring
Like glad-hearted children together.

Summer Woods

O I am tired of painted roofs and soft and silken
floors,
And long for wind-blown canopies of crimson gulmohurs

O I am tired of strife and song and festivals and
fame,
And long to fly where cassia-woods are breaking into
flame.

Love, come with me where koels call from flowering
glade and glen.
Far from the toil and weariness, the praise and prayers
of men.

O let us fling all care away, and lie alone and dream
'Neath tangled boughs of tamarind and molsari and
neem!

And bind our brows with jasmine sprays and play
on carven flutes,
To wake the slumbering serpent-kings among the
banyan roots.

And roam at fall of eventide along the river's brink.
And bathe in water-lily pools where golden panthers
drink!

You and I together. Love, in the deep blossoming
woods
Engirt with low-voiced silences and gleaming solitudes.

Companions of the lustrous dawn, gay comrades of
the night.
Like Krishna and like Radhika, encompassed with
delight.

Ashoka Blossom

If a lovely maiden's foot
Treads on the Ashoka root.
Its glad branches sway and swell,—
So our eastern legends tell,—
Into gleaming flower.
Vivid clusters golden-red
To adorn her brow or bed
Or her marriage bower.
If your glowing foot be prest
O'er the secrets of my breast,
Love, my dreaming head would wake,
And its joyous fancies break
Into lyric bloom
To enchant the passing world
With melodious leaves unfurled
And their wild perfume.

The Offering

Were beauty mine, Beloved, I would bring it
Like a rare blossom to Love's glowing shrine;
Were dear youth mine, Beloved, I would fling it
Like a rich pearl into Love's lustrous wine.

Were greatness mine. Beloved, I would offer
Such radiant gifts of glory and of fame.
Like camphor and like curds to pour and proffer
Before Love's bright and sacrificial flame.

But I have naught save my heart's deathless passion
That craves no recompense divinely sweet,
Content to wait in proud and lowly fashion,
And kiss the shadow of Love's passing feet.

If You Call Me

If you call me I will come
Swifter, O my Love,
Than a trembling forest deer
Or a panting dove,
Swifter than a snake that flies
To the charmer's thrall . . .
If you call me I will come
Fearless what befall.
If you call me, I will come
Swifter than desire.
Swifter than the lightning's feet
Shod with plumes of fire.
Life's dark tides may roll between,
Or Death's deep chasms divide—
If you call me I will come
Fearless what betide.

SPEECHES

Introduction to Speeches

Over the years, Sarojini Naidu was a part of many gatherings where she was invited to speak. She had a chance to address a range of people, from college students, to disenfranchised women, Indians living overseas and political party members. Ever eloquent, she would find a way to connect to each audience with a specific anecdote that they could relate to. The selected speeches include some of her most well-known pieces— 'The Education of Indian Women' and 'The Battle of Freedom Is Over', which was broadcast on the All India Radio on 15 August 1947. All of these reveal her love for the country, vehement opposition to inequality of any kind, her belief in the youth, and her valiant fight for the right of women and unity among the citizens of India. Each speech has a few lines of description before it to set the context.

True Brotherhood

The following is a lecture delivered at a public meeting held under the auspices of the Historical Society, Pachaiyappa's College, Madras in 1903:

You know that you are provincial—and you are more limited than that—because your horizon is bounded almost by your city, your own community, your own sub-caste, your own college, your own homes, your own relations, your own self (loud cheers). I know I am speaking rightly, because I also in my earlier youth was afflicted with the same sort of short-sightedness of the love. Having travelled, having conceived, having hoped, having enlarged my love, having widened my sympathies, having come in contact with different races, different communities, different religions, different civilizations, friends, my vision is clear. I have no prejudice of race, creed, caste or colour. Though, as is supposed, every Brahman is an aristocrat by instinct, I am a real democrat, because to me there is no difference between a king on his throne and a beggar in the street. And until you, students, have acquired and mastered that spirit of brotherhood, do not believe it possible that you will ever cease to be provincial, that you will cease to be sectarian—if I may use such a word—that you will ever be national. If it were otherwise, there should have been no necessity for all those resolutions in the Social Conference yesterday. I look to you and to the generation that is passing; it is the young that would have the courage to cast aside that bondage to make it impossible for the Social Conference of ten years hence to proclaim its disgrace in the manner in which it was proclaimed yesterday and in which I took part (continued cheers). Students, if facilities come in your way, travel; because the knowledge that comes from living contact with men and minds, the inestimable culture that comes through interchange of ideas, can never be equalled and certainly not surpassed by that knowledge between the covers of text books. You read the poems of Shelley on Liberty. You read the lecture of Keats on the Brotherhood of Man, but do you put them all in practice? Reading is one thing. It is a very different thing to put it into practice by your deeds. It is difficult to follow in reality the proverb that all men are brethren. Therefore, to you, young men, we look for the fulfilment of the dreams that we have dreamed. To you we look to rectify the mistakes we have made. To you we look to redeem the pledges we have given to posterity. I beg of you, young men, nay, I enjoin upon you that duty that you dare not, if you are men, separate from your hearts and mind and spirit. I say that it is not your pride that you are a Madrasi, that it is not your pride that you are a Brahman, that it is not your pride you belong to the

South of India, that it is not your pride you are a Hindu, but that it is your pride that you are an Indian. I was born in Bengal. I belong to the Madras Presidency. In a Muhammadan city I was brought up and married, and there I lived; still I am neither a Bengali, nor a Madrasi, nor a Hyderabadi, but I am an Indian (cheers), not a Hindu, not a Brahman, but an Indian to whom my Muhammadan brother is as dear and as precious as my Hindu brother. I was brought up in a home that would never have tolerated the least spirit of difference in the treatment given to people of different classes. There you will find that genuine, spontaneous love shown to them. I was brought up in a home over which presided one of the greatest men of India and who was an embodiment of all great lores and an ideal of truth, of love, of justice, of patriotism. That great teacher of India had come to us to give immortal inspiration. That is a home of Indians and not of Hindus or Brahmans. It is because my beloved father said 'Be not limited even to the Indians, but let it be your pride that you are a citizen of the world,' that I should love my country. I am ready to lay down my life for the welfare of all India. I beg of you, my brothers, not to limit your love only to India, because it is better to aim at the sky, it is better that your ideals of patriotism should extend to the welfare of the world and not be limited to the prosperity of India and so to achieve that prosperity for your country; because, if the ideals be only for the prosperity of your country, it would end where it began, by being a profit to your own community and very probably to your own self. You have inherited great dreams. You have had great duties laid upon you. You have been bequeathed legacies for whose suffrage and whose growth and accumulation you are responsible. It does not matter where you are and who you are. Even a sweeper of streets can be a patriot. You can find in him a moralizing spirit that can inspire your mind. There is not one of you who is so humble and so insignificant that can evade the duties that belong to you, that are predestined to you and which nobody but you can perform. Therefore each of you is bound to dedicate his life to the up-lifting of his country.

The Education of Indian Women

It seems to me a paradox, at once touched with humour and tragedy, that on the very threshold of the twentieth century, it should still be necessary for us to stand upon public platforms and pass resolutions in favour of what is called female education in India—in all places in India, which, at the beginning of the first century, was already ripe with civilization and had contributed to the world's progress radiant examples of women of the highest genius and the widest culture. But as by some irony of evolution the paradox stands to our shame, it is time for us to consider how best we can remove such a reproach, how we can best achieve something more fruitful than the passing of empty resolutions in favour of female education from year to year. At this great moment of stress and striving, when the Indian races are seeking for the ultimate unity of a common national ideal, it is well for us to remember that the success of the whole movement lies centred in what is known as the woman question. It is not you but we who are the true nation-builders. But it seems to me that there is not even an unanimous acceptance of the fact that the education of women is an essential factor in the process of nation-building. Many of you will remember that, some years ago, when Mrs. Satthianadhan first started *The Indian Ladies' Magazine*, a lively correspondence went on as to whether we should or should not educate our women. The women themselves with one voice pleaded their own cause most eloquently, but when it came to the man, there was division in the camp. Many men doubtless proved themselves true patriots by proving themselves the true friends of education for the mothers of the people. But others were there who took fright at the very word. 'What,' they cried, 'educate our women? What, then, will become of the comfortable domestic ideals as exemplified by the luscious "halwa" and the savoury "omelette"?' Others, again, were neither 'for Jove nor for Jehovah,' but were for compromise, bringing forward a whole syllabus of compromises. 'Teach this,' they said, 'and not that.' But, my friends, in the matter of education you cannot flay thus far and no further. Neither can you say to the winds of Heaven 'Blow not where ye list,' nor forbid the waves to cross their boundaries, nor yet the human soul to soar beyond the bounds of arbitrary limitations. The word education is the worst misunderstood word in any language. The Italians, who are an imaginative people, with their subtle instinct for the inner meaning of words, have made a positive difference between instruction and education and we should do well to accept and acknowledge that difference. Instruction being merely the accumulation of knowledge might, indeed, lend itself to conventional definition, but education is an immeasurable, beautiful, indispensable atmosphere in which we live and move and have our being. Does one man dare to deprive another of his birthright to God's pure air which nourishes his body? How, then, shall a man dare to deprive a human soul of its immemorial inheritance of liberty and life? And yet, my friends, man has so dared in the case of Indian women. That is why you men of India are today what you are: because your fathers, in depriving your mothers of that immemorial birthright, have robbed you, their sons, of your just inheritance. Therefore, I charge you, restore to your women their ancient rights, for, as I have said, it is we, and not you, who are the real nation-builders, and without our active co-operation at all points of progress, all your Congresses and Conferences are in vain. Educate your women and the nation will take care of itself, for it is true today as it was yesterday and will be to the end of human life that the hand that rocks the cradle is the power that rules the world.

Reminiscences of Mr. Gokhale

After Gopal Krishna Gokhale's death, Mrs Sarojini Naidu wrote a piece in the Bombay Chronicle *as her way of remembering him:*

My personal association with Mr. Gokhale commenced, as it ended, with a written message. It had fallen to me to propose the resolution on the education of women at the Calcutta Session of the All-India Social Conference of 1906; and something in my speech moved him sufficiently to pass me these hurried and cordial sentences which, unworthy as I know myself of such generous appreciation, I venture to transcribe, since they struck the key-note of all our future intercourse. 'May I take the liberty,' he wrote, 'to offer you my most respectful and enthusiastic congratulations? Your speech was more than an intellectual treat of the highest order. We all felt for the moment to be lifted to a higher plane.'

An acquaintance begun on such a happy note of sympathy, grew and ripened at last into a close and lovely comradeship which I counted among the crowning honours of my life. And though it was not without its poignant moments of brief and bitter estrangement, our friendship was always radiant, both with the joy of spiritual refreshment, and the quickening challenge of intellectual discussion and dissent. Above all, there was the ever-deepening bond of our common love for the motherland; and, for a short space, there was alone the added tie of a tender dependence, infinitely touching and child-like on such comfort and companionship as I, with my own broken health, could render him through long weeks of suffering and distress in a foreign land.

Between 1907 and 1911, it was my good fortune to meet him several times, chiefly during my flying visits to Bombay, but also on different occasions, in Madras, Poona, and Delhi. After each meeting, I would always carry away the memory of some fervent and stirring word of exhortation to yield my life to the service of India. And, even in the midst of the crowded activities of those epoch-making years, he found leisure to send me, now and then, a warm message of approval, of encouragement, when any poem or speech or action of mine chanced to please him or the frequent rumours of my failing health caused him anxiety or alarm.

But it was not till the beginning of 1912, when I spent a few weeks in Calcutta with my father, that any real intimacy was established between us. 'Hitherto I have always caught you on the wing,' he said, 'now I will cage you long enough to grasp your true spirits.' It was in the course of the long and delightful conversations of this period that I began to comprehend the intrinsic and versatile greatness of the man, and to marvel by what austere and fruitful process he was able to reconcile and assimilate the complex and often conflicting qualities of his essentially dual personality into so supreme an achievement of single-hearted patriotism. It was to me a valuable lesson in human psychology to study the secret of this rich and paradoxical nature. There was the outer man as the world knew and esteemed him, with his precise and brilliant and subtle intellect, his unrivalled gifts of political analysis and synthesis, his flawless and relentless mastery and use of the consummate logic of coordinated facts and figures, his courteous but inexorable candour in opposition, his patient dignity and courage in honourable compromise, the breadth and restraint, the vigour and veracity of his far-reaching statesmanship, the lofty simplicities and sacrifices of his daily life. And breaking through the veils of his many self-repressions was the inner man that revealed himself to me in all his intense, impassioned hunger for human kinship and affection, in all the tumult and longing, the agony of doubt and ecstasy of faith of the born idealist, perpetually seeking some unchanging reality in a world full of shifting disillusion and despair. In him I felt that both the practical, strenuous worker and the mystic dreamer of dreams were harmonized by the age-long discipline of his Brahminical ancestry which centuries before had evolved the spirit of the Bhagavad Gita and defined true Yoga as Wisdom in Action. But even he could not escape the limitations of the inheritance. Wide and just as were his recognitions of all human claims to equality, he had nevertheless hidden away, perhaps unsuspected, something of that conservative pride of his Brahminical descent which instinctively resented the least question of its ancient monopoly of power. One little instance of this weakness—if I may use the word—occurs to me. At the All-India Conference which was held in Calcutta at the end of 1911, in the course of an address on the so-called Depressed Classes, I happened to have remarked that the denial of their equal human rights and opportunities of life was largely due to the tyranny of arrogant Brahmans in the past. My father, who was also present at the meeting, noted and ironically rallied me on the phrase which appealed to both his sense of humour and equity. But to my surprise, I found that Mr. Gokhale regarded the word 'arrogant' almost as a personal affront! 'It was no doubt a brave and beautiful speech,' he said in a tone of reproach, 'but you sometimes use harsh, bold phrases.' Soon after discussing an allied topic, he burst out saying, 'You—in spite of yourself—you are typically Hindu in spirit. You begin with a ripple and end in eternity.' 'But,' I answered, a little nettled, 'when have I ever disclaimed my heritage?'

Another conversation of these weeks stands out with special significance in the light of coming events. one morning, a little despondent and sick at heart about national affairs in general, he suddenly asked me, 'What is your outlook for India?' 'One of Hope,' I replied. 'What is your vision of our immediate future?' 'The Hindu-Muslim Unity in less than five years,' I told him with joyous conviction. 'Child,' he said, with a note of yearning sadness in his voice, 'you are a poet, but you hope too much. It will not come in your life-time or in mine. But keep your faith and work if you can.' In March of the following year, I met him for a few minutes only at a large party in Bombay given by Sir Pherozeshah Mehta for the members of the Royal Commission. I had recently brought out a new book of verses which just then happily for me was attracting some attention and applause. And Mr. Gokhale's short conversation with me was very characteristic of his attitude of distrust towards such things. 'Does the flame still burn brightly?' he questioned. 'Brighter than ever,' I answered. But he shook his head doubtfully and a little sternly. 'I wonder,' he said, 'I wonder how the storm of such long duration will withstand excessive adulation and success.'

A week later, it was my unique privilege to attend and address the new historic session of the Muslim League which met in Lucknow on the 22nd March, to adopt a new Constitution which sounded the key-note of loyal co-operation with the sister community in all matters of national welfare and progress. The unanimous acclamation with which it was carried by both the older and younger schools of Mussalman politicians marked a new era and inaugurated a new standard in the history of modern Indian affairs. From Lucknow I travelled, almost without a break, direct to Poona, where I was due on the 25th, and on the morning of the 26th, I walked across with the Hon. Mr. Paranjpye from Fergusson

College to the Servants of India Society. I found the world-famous leader of the Indian National Congress weak and suffering from a relapse of his old illness, but busy scanning the journals that were full of comments and criticisms of the Muslim League and its new ideals. 'Ah,' he cried with outstretched hands when he saw me, 'have you come to tell me that your vision was true?' and he began to question me over and over again with a breathless eagerness that seemed almost impatient of my words about the real underlying spirit of the Conference. His weary and pain-worn face lighted up with pleasure when I assured him that, so far at least as the younger men were concerned, it was not an instinct of mere political expediency but one of genuine conviction and a growing consciousness of wider and graver national responsibility that had prompted them to stretch out so frankly and generously the hand of good fellowship to the Hindus, and I hoped that the coming Congress would respond to it with equal, if not even greater, cordiality. 'So far as it lies in my power,' he answered, 'it shall be done.' After an hour or so, I found him exhausted with the excitement of the happy news I had brought him from so far, but he insisted on my returning to complete my visit to him that afternoon.

When I went back to the Servants of India Society in the evening, I found a strangely transformed Mr. Gokhale, brisk and smiling, a little pale, but without any trace of the morning's languor and depression. 'What,' I almost screamed as he was preparing to lead the way upstairs, 'surely you cannot mean to mount all those steps, you are too ill.' He laughed, 'You have put new hope into me,' he said, 'I feel strong enough to face life and work again.' Presently, his sister and two charming daughters joined us for half an hour on the broad terrace with its peaceful view over sunset hills and valleys, and we talked of pleasant and passing things. This was my first and only glimpse and realization of the personal domestic side of this lonely and impersonal worker. After their departure, we sat quietly in the gathering twilight till his golden voice, stirred by some deep emotion, broke the silence with golden words of counsel and admonition, so grand, so solemn and so inspiring, that they have never ceased to thrill me. He spoke of the unequalled happiness and privilege of service for India. 'Stand here with me,' he said, 'with the stars and hills for witness and in their presence consecrate your life and your talent, your song and your speech, your thought and your dream to the motherland. O poet, see visions from the hill-tops and spread abroad the message of hope to the toilers in the valleys.' As I took my leave of him, he said again to this humble messenger of happy tidings: 'You have given me new hope, new faith, new courage. Tonight I shall rest. I shall sleep with a heart at peace.'

Two months later, early in June after an absence of fifteen years, I found myself in London once more, and among the many friends who greeted me on my arrival was the familiar figure of Mr. Gokhale in wholly unfamiliar European garments and—yes—actually an

English top hat. I stared at him for a moment. 'Where,'
I asked him, 'is your rebellious turban?' But I soon got
accustomed to this new phase of my old friend, to a social
Gokhale who attended parties and frequented theatres,
played bridge and entertained ladies at dinner on the
terrace of the National Liberal Club, a far cry from the
terrace of the Servants of India Society.

In spite of his uncertain health, he was very busy
throughout the summer with his work on the Royal
Commission and his anxious pre-occupations with Indian
affairs in South Africa, then threatening an acute crisis.
But he would often come to see me where I was staying at
the house of Sir Krishna Gupta. Mr. Gokhale had a great
fancy for cherries, and I always took care to provide a
liberal supply whenever he was expected. 'Every man has
his price,' I would tease him, 'and yours is cherries.' One
day, at the end of July, sitting over a dish of ripe red cherries,
I broached the subject of a delicate mission which I had
undertaken on behalf of the London Indian Association,
a new student organization that had only a few weeks
previously been founded by Mr. M.A. Jinnah with the
active and eager support of Indian students in London.
Their earnest endeavour was to provide a permanent centre
to focus the scattered student life in London and to build
up such staunch tradition of co-operation and fellowship
that this young association might eventually grow into a
perfect miniature and model of the federated India of the
future, the India of their dreams, and it was their ardent
desire to start on their new mission of service with a

word of sympathy and blessing from this incomparable friend and servant of India. At first, a firm refusal of my request backed by the strict prohibition of his doctors of all undue strain and fatigue somewhat daunted me. But I had a little rashly more or less pledged my word that he would speak, and I redoubled my persuasions. 'You not only defy all laws of health yourself,' he grumbled, 'but incite me also to disobedience and revolt.' 'Besides,' and his eyes flashed for a moment, 'what right had you to pledge your word for me?' 'The right,' I told him, 'to demand from you at all costs a message of hope for the young generation.' A few days later, on the 2nd August, he delivered a magnificent inaugural address at Caxton Hall in the presence of a large and enthusiastic audience of students, and set before them those sublime lessons of patriotism and self-sacrifice which he alone so signally, among the men of his generation, was competent to teach with authority and grace.

Shortly afterwards he left for India to wage his brave and glorious battle in the cause of his suffering compatriots in South Africa. And though now his health was finally ruined beyond all chance of recovery, it was with the rapture of victorious martyrdom that he wrote from his sick-bed, about the end of December, to tell me how prompt and splendid had been the response of a truly United India to the call of her gallant heroes fighting for right and justice in a far-off land.

On his return to England in the spring of 1914, his condition was so precarious as to cause his friends and physicians the gravest concern; and at first he was confined entirely to bed. But with his ever-gracious kindness towards me, he paid me a visit on the very day he was permitted to leave his room, as I was then too ill to go and see him. 'Why should a song-bird like you have a broken wing,' he murmured a little sadly, and presently told me that he had just received his own death-warrant at the hands of his doctors. 'With the utmost care,' he said, 'they think, I might perhaps live for three years longer.' But in his calm and thoughtful manner there was no sign of selfish rebellion or fear—only an infinite regret for his unfinished service to India.

But soon, I was well enough to accompany him on the short motor drives that were his sole form of recreation, and on mild days, as we sat in the soft sunshine under the budding trees of Kensington Gardens he would talk to me with that sure instinct of his for choice and graphic phrases that lent his conversation so much distinction and charm. 'Give me a corner of your brain that I can call my own,' he would say. And in that special corner that was his I treasure many memorable sayings. I learnt to wonder not merely at the range and variety of his culture but at his fastidious preferences for what Charles Lamb has called the delicacies of fine literature. He had also an almost romantic curiosity towards the larger aspect of life and death and destiny, and a quick apprehension of the mysterious forces that govern the main springs of human feeling and experience. One day, a little wistfully, he said, 'Do you know, I feel that an abiding sadness underlies all that unfailing brightness of yours? Is it because you have come so near death that its shadows still cling to you?' 'No,' I answered, 'I have come so near life that its fires have burnt me.' But, like a humming bird, his heart would always return with swift and certain flight to the one immutable passion of his life, his love for that India which to him was mistress and mother, goddess and child in one. He would speak of the struggles and disappointments of his early days, the triumphs and failures, the rewards and renunciations of his later years, his vision of India and her ultimate goal, her immediate value as an Imperial asset, and her appointed place and purpose in the wider counsels and responsibilities of the Empire. He spoke too of his work and his colleagues, the Royal Commission, the Viceregal Council and the National Congress; and though to the end he remained a better judge of human situations rather than of individuals, I was struck with the essential fairness of his estimates which seemed in one luminous phrase to reveal the true measure of a man. Of one he said that 'He can mould heroes out of common clay,' of another that 'He has fine sincerity, a little marred by hasty judgment,' of yet another: 'He has true stuff in him and that freedom from all sectarian prejudice which will make him the best ambassador of the Hindu-Muslim unity.' Of a fourth, 'He has made those sacrifices which entitle him to be heard.'

Of the many pressing matters that occupied his mind at that time, there were four which to him were of absorbing interest. His scheme for compulsory education, which he felt was the only solid basis on which to found any lasting national progress; the Hindu-Mussalman question which, he said, could be most effectively solved if the leaders of the sister communities would deal in a spirit of perfect unison with certain fundamental problems of equal and urgent importance to both the high privilege and heavy responsibility of the young generation whose function it was to grapple with more immense and vital issues than his generation had been called upon to face; and of course the future of the Servants of India Society, which was the actual embodiment of all his dreams and devotion for India.

These open-air conversations, however, came to a speedy end. He suddenly grew worse and was forbidden to leave his room or to receive visitors. But I was fortunate enough to be allowed to see him almost daily for a few hours till his departure to Vichy. In his whimsical way he would call me the best of all his prescriptions. To my usual query on crossing the threshold of his sick-room, 'Well, am I to be a stimulant or a sedative today?', his invariable reply was 'Both.' And this one word most adequately summed up the need of his sinking heart and overburdened brain through these anxious and critical weeks.

The interval between his first and second visits to Vichy he spent in a quiet little cottage at Twickenham as the guest and neighbour of Mr. and Mrs. Ratan Tata, to whom the nation already owes so many debts of gratitude, and the monotony of the long hours of his temporary and interrupted convalescence was often brightened by the presence of friends whose visits to him were really pilgrimages, and sustained by the devoted attendance of Dr. Jivraj Mehta who has since won such proud academic honours, and of whom Mr. Gokhale more than once said: 'He will go far and be a leader of men.'

From Vichy he wrote, 'Here, in this intense mental solitude, I have come upon the bedrock truths of life and must learn to adjust myself to their demands.' The outbreak of War in August brought him back to England a little prematurely. But though his health had obviously improved, and he was better able to stand the strain of his arduous work on the Royal Commission, he seemed oppressed with a sharp and sudden sense of exile in the midst of an alien civilization and people. He was haunted by a deep nostalgia which he himself could not explain, not merely for the wonted physical scenes and surroundings but for the spiritual texts and tongues of his ancestral land. His conversation during these days was steeped in allusions to the old Sanskrit writers whose mighty music was in his very blood.

The last occasion on which I saw him was on the 8th of October, two days before I sailed for India. Something, may be, of the autumnal sadness of fallen leaves and growing mists had passed into his mood; or, may be, he felt the foreshadowing of the wings of Death. But as he bade me farewell, he said, 'I do not think we shall meet again. If you live, remember your life is dedicated to the service of the country. My work is done.'

Early in December, shortly after his arrival from Europe, he wrote to complain of the 'scurvy trick' fate had played him in a renewal of his old trouble; but succeeding letters reported returning strength and ability to work again. In the last letter written the day before his fatal illness, he spoke of his health being now stationary and of his coming visit to Delhi. But it was otherwise ordained. As the poet says, 'True as the peach to its ripening taste is destiny to her hour.' His predestined hour had already struck. On the 19th February, the self-same stars that he had invoked one year ago to witness the consecration of a life to the service of India kept vigil over the passing of this great saint and soldier of national righteousness. And of him surely, in another age and in another land were the prophetic words uttered—'Greater love hath no man than this, that a man lay down his life for his friends.'

The Ideal of Civic Life

At the fourteenth anniversary of the Young Men's Literary Association, Guntur, held on 5 July 1915, Sarojini Naidu delivered the following speech:

Mr President, Ladies, Gentlemen, and my Friends the Students—It is of course in accordance with the right of etiquette of the moment and the occasion to say how deeply honoured I am by being asked to address you on this auspicious occasion, but, believe me when I say it is not merely in fulfilment of a conventional point of etiquette, but because I feel it with all my heart to be a source of not merely pleasure but honour and privilege to me to be asked to meet you this evening when you are gathered here in your hundreds to celebrate the fourteenth anniversary of the institution which, if it has not already, will, I hope, in time, become the very heart- beat of the life of this great and increasingly prosperous and progressive city. As I was listening to the report so clearly written and effectively read by the earnest secretary, I was looking around on this ocean of faces representing all generations that have hitherto contributed to the progress of Gantur and who are going in future to contribute something better than their old generations could offer because of their more limited opportunities.

This morning a most earnest member of this society said to me that a few students started it some years ago which was the centre of their own life and that with them it grew up. As students expanded into larger life, they expanded it with their growth into manhood from its infancy of earlier days. It seems to me a symbolic thing because what one would say to impress on the growing generation that they must carry into expanded intellectual public life all those dreams and all ambitions of dreams. They are merely dreams to them because they are too young to realize them, but when once they had crossed the threshold of manhood and come into the horizon of responsibility and opportunity, they are to transmute their dreams into deeds; so the origin of this association seems to me to carry its own guarantee of unbroken continuity. Today, after 14 years, the men who started it as students for the use of themselves carried it giving it the best energies, vitality and sacrificing many things, personal pleasures, wealth and comfort because they wished it to grow and become a real heart-beat of the country. Do you not think that it is not merely a prophecy but an actual guarantee of promise almost fulfilled. Today I do not wish to speak to those who were students 14 years ago when they started this institution. But I wish to speak to those who are going to be the future sustainers of this institution, those who are going to be the inheritors of all the active achievements and even in a greater degree of all the dreams that we dreamt 14 years ago. But I want to tell them what it means to be citizens—the type of citizens. They must be an ideal for the world to follow. Curiously enough, it is during the last 14 years that the by-gone generation of students were dreaming dreams and that the institution is a focus of all their dreaming, discussion, of all their hopes of the future. I, too, was young, dreaming dreams, and I too started carrying my dreams not focussing them in one institution but going on from place to place to speak for the younger generation, to tell them how real were their dreams and how it was possible to realize those dreams. Today, after 14 years of speaking to young men and young women all over the country, I come to this centre of the Andhra country to speak with the citizens of the Andhra Province. I want to tell you what the ideal of civic life is for you. All over India today there is a new spirit awake that thrills the heart of the young generation from end to end, from north and south, east and west, the spirit that is called the renaissance, not a new spirit but a spirit reborn and revitalized in the past that held exactly such ideals and dreams that taught by precept and example, such principles as you wish to fulfil in your life for the service of your country, whether you go to Bengal and speak with young men with the passionate spirit of ideals, whether you go to the Mahratta country and see those intellectual youths with their spirit focussed and ready for any sacrifice, and whether you go to South India and see those vigorous and intellectual types of eyes drinking every word set before them, you realize the young spirit is the same, though it speaks in different vernaculars. Vernaculars are different, races are different, castes are different; but the thing that makes you all is the one spirit that is abroad today. You know that the students' movement in Bengal is so much a vital part of the everyday life of the people, that one cannot conceive of the future, not even today. In Bengal, the students' ideal fervour, and capacity for service does not count the most inspiring factor in the national life. You go to Bombay, the second to London in its commercial greatness, and you find that the greatness and the glory of Bombay does not lie in its beautiful buildings, not in the glory of merchant princes and women hung about in diamonds, but rather it is in the movement to be carried in the small scale of brotherhood because the force of it was so strong and it answers so strongly the need of young generation. It has become today the most representative thing of the new spirit of Bombay. The historian writing of the future of Bombay will not speak of the palaces on the Malabar Hill, or of the factories vomiting smoke, or of the motor cars, but rather of those young students very many of them ill clad but whose races shine like lamp-lights dazzling by night. Take my native state—Hyderabad— the new spirit is awake there in the city and it is so awake that already it has solved without any consciousness that it has done so, the greatest problem that all our political reformers are trying to solve, i.e, the question of Hindu-Muslim unity, and that is the greatest contribution to the future of India that the young generation can make in such places where there exists a problem and an imminent necessity for the solution. That the young generation has done already in the city of Hyderabad. And now coming to the Andhra Province, will you believe me that it fills and thrills me with pride to say that, while even in those great Presidencies that have achieved so much I have even found more the light of rhetoric than of action, I find that within a few years after the Andhra Provinces began to wake and set their ideals before them and assert their individual entity because they wished to contribute their characteristic share and their united right to contribute to the future of the federated culture in India (shouts of joy) in these few years we find not merely rhetoric from platform from people loving rhetoric but hard work, self-sacrificing devotion, enthusiasm and daily and early sacrifice and personal service. That is what I have found in the Andhra country. It was my great privilege to go to Masulipatam for the fifth anniversary of the National College there. I found there and since then I have come very intimately in contact with some of the older and younger men who represented the spirit of what I called the Andhra renaissance. Once more it has been my privilege to come closer to the heart-beat of that Andhra spirit. I was in Pithapur two days ago. There I found not only men but women who began to realize their inviolable right to co-operate with men in re-establishing the historic distinction of their province. They say, 'All that we want to do in our little sphere is the little practicable work which is to offer a beautiful and priceless offering to the feet of our motherland.' That is the spirit in which the women of the Andhra Province are working.

What I want to bring to these young citizens before me is this. That it is your duty—you who are in a state of apprenticeship and who are learning the knowledge from the text-books. You will have in a few years to learn in a more difficult university lessons that no man will teach you by the hand. Many of the dreams you dream today so light-heartedly will taste bitter in your mouth because you will find so much opposition and so many difficulties. Be true to yourself. I want each one of you to be a worthy worshipper of that great name that is representative of the past ideals that moulded your historic dynasties. It is to realize by the building up of character, however great the opposition in life may be, however obscure your life may be, however insignificant and unknown the position in which you live, it does not matter; each of you can make yourself a worthy devotee of that flame of spirit. Each of you in doing so will be doing the best possible service to your country and to your race in the world. It is the best way in which you will be able to serve humanity by building up these trait of character that have distinguished your people, vis. valour, intellectual capacity, and spiritual devotion.

Passing on she said: The thing which is very necessary for us to remember is that as modern civilization progresses, as the world becomes more and more international in giving and receiving enlightenment, we are absorbing from other countries as we are giving to other countries. With such ideas, such treasures of knowledge and experience of wider horizon and scientific thought, the responsibility of personal service becomes greater.

Life is more complex. I ask you to dedicate your life to this cause, to make your lights ready to be kindled at the flame of devotion, to serve your country worthily. I do not say to you to become teachers to preach or politicians by this or by that. Whatever your sphere in life is, however small you are, remember, you are an indispensable unit in making up that vast social organization which makes the country a nation. I want you all to remember that the greatness of a country will not lie in its great men, but in its average good men, who realized the daily life of purity, truth, courage in overcoming such obstacles that stand in the way of progress by giving equal opportunities to all human beings, of all castes and creeds and not to withhold from any man or woman his or her God-given, inviolable right to live to the fullest capacity. That is the meaning of social reform. Give education to low castes. Do give to your women, who are co-operators with you in your generation, for you are building the national character, such a right to qualify themselves for the high and great responsibility of motherhood. In this institution, the most valuable asset—an asset more valuable than all the funds of zemindars—is the actual spirit of service on the part of the members of the society.

Finance is one of the wants of the institution; it seems to me it is a supreme want. If today I have come from so far, loving to see the spirit that animates you, you will let me go away with the hope that this institution will not die simply from want of this help of money (cries of emphatic 'no'). I beg all of you to rise as one man to make this institution really a representation of the ideals that you believe—the ideals that you wish your children and children's children to inherit.

Women in National Life

Mrs Sarojini Naidu, in proposing the Resolution on the women in national life in the Indian National Social Conference held at Bombay on 30 December 1915, said:

Mr. President, Brother-Delegates, Ladies and Gentlemen, this resolution that I have to propose, although it came third on the list of resolutions had to be changed for my personal convenience; it is a happy thought to have put it first because it embodies a resolution that deals with the most important problems of our social progress, and that is the education of our women. As I was listening to that inspiring and stirring address by our revered President a little while ago, it seemed to me that no woman could have pleaded the cause of women with a greater conviction of her rights and her privileges and her destiny in the future as an unbroken historic tradition from the past; and whatever I might say speaking as a woman, and an Indian woman, for my sisters, cannot possibly carry the same weight with you, because it will not go from me with that tradition of sacrifice, that living reality of daily service in the cause of women which Prof. Karve has embodied in his life. But when I look around me today and consider that ten years ago in Calcutta from the platform of the Social Conference I pleaded for the education of women, there was not a gathering of women quite as much as the gathering present here today, and that itself is sufficient to prove that within the last tea years not only the men but those more intimately and essentially concerned the women themselves, have begun to realise the cause of a new spirit which is nothing but a renaissance of the old spirit which gave to India those Gargis, Maitrayis, those Savitris and Sitas of whom Mr. Bhupendra Nath Basu spoke a little while ago. And if I speak to you today in favour and in support of this educational policy for our women, for a more liberal grant from the authorities, for more co-operation from our men, I will demand from my sisters not merely that liberality of endowment that we ask from Government, not merely the co-operation from our brothers, but from them their pledge of individual and personal consecration to this great cause; I will demand from every sister of mine her personal dedication to this cause, because it is not from Government or even from the co-operation of the manhood of the country that the solution of this question will come. It is not from them that you will get the impetus to wipe off the stain from our national history, but rather from the womanhood of India which is suffering from a wrong. My reproach is to the women of India, and though I make it in their presence I do it as a woman speaking to women, and do it with the fullest realization of what I am saying because I feel the voices of millions of my sons crying out from one end to another end. Let the womanhood of the country wake and work. Let us strengthen the hands of our men. Those prayers that we prayed, those thoughts that we uttered in the thousands gathered together year after year, passing resolutions, are but the sincerest desire of every member of the society that has the interest of the country at heart. When I was in Europe a little more than a year ago after 15 years of absence from the continent of progress, during my last visit to Europe, what struck me in that great continent of rapid changes, of evolution going on at a rate that one can hardly calculate by the hands of a clock, that it was the womanhood of Europe that had begun to realize the full measure of its strength, the full height of its responsibility, the full sanctity and seriousness of its duty in the nation-building of Europe. Everywhere I found that women of all classes that had been considered luxury-loving had become transmuted into servers of the country's good. Women, whose chief assets 15 years ago might have been the jewels or the ornaments, had for their asset now that living sympathy, that personal service to the poor, that share of responsibility in solving the great problems of the generation every nation is called upon to solve. And when I came back to India a year ago, the first thing that struck me after nearly two years of absence was that the womanhood of India was beginning to wake in an unmistakable way. I have come in contact with thousands and thousands of women in every part of India and the same message comes forth that unity of Indian womanhood, if it is desired to achieve it, is to be found in the national service.

When I was in the Kistna and Godavari districts it surprised me to find how in that country where there is a new movement to re-establish a national consciousness, the women stood side by side with their men in every detail, and not merely in the abstract ideals of achieving that regeneration, that renaissance of the Andhra country. Everywhere I found that wherever there was a school to be started or a mission for social service, wherever there was a movement to bring back to the Indian consciousness that sense of national dignity, that sense of national responsibility, the women of the Andhra country stood side by side with their men. In Bengal, I found in that sweet country, where the very educational ardour is transmuted in devotion for the country, there I found man and woman ready to bring his or her life like a lotus flower in consecration to the feet of Bharat Varsha. In this Presidency where every community is represented not in minorities but in equal proportions, of strength and of prosperity, where there is that wholesome stimulus for every good work, I find the spirit of the womanhood of this Presidency, the women of the Maharashtra, the women of the Zoroastrian community and the women who say Yah Allah, Yah Allah of Muhammadanism, though they are divided by race and creed and religion, they are yet indivisible, one by the realization of their common womanhood, and they are one by the consciousness of their common duty which is the duty of every woman whose destiny it is to create the generation of the citizens of tomorrow, and if this resolution comes into a Conference like this it comes with the whole-hearted support of this great gathering of women who, though great with their numbers, are still only a fraction of that large majority who are thinking and desiring and hoping and struggling to bring back to India that dignity, that liberty, that deliverance from evil, that freedom of all social laws which comes of education. They are trying here, as elsewhere, as all true women must, to realise that their share in co-operating with their men is the only condition of national regeneration. They are beginning to realize that it is not only by having large ideals that this service is to be achieved but rather by analyzing those great ideals into their component practical parts, and every one taking up a little share of practical service, and all those ideals and all those visions of tomorrow are centred round this supreme question of the education of women. Other national questions come and go. They are the result of the changing time-spirit, but the one question that has never changed since the beginning of time itself, and life itself, is the duty of womanhood, the influence of womanhood, the sanctity of womanhood, the simple womanhood as the divinity of God upon earth, the responsibility of womanhood in shaping the divinity into daily life. Friends, two nights ago I was speaking in Poona at the All-India Muhammadan Educational Conference, and I was the one representative

of my sect in the midst of hundreds of Muhammadan
men, and I was asked to thank on behalf of those women
who are separated from their men, not merely by virtue
of sect, but rather divided from them by tradition and
custom. It was I who said, Oh men, unless and until you
give to your women all those equal privileges that form
the highest and noblest teaching of your great nation-
builder and Prophet you will not attain that regeneration
of your race that renaissance of Islamic glory, and today
in the presence of this great gathering chiefly of Hindus, I
say, Oh friends. Oh brothers. Oh sisters, look back to the
past and look forward to the future, and let your future
draw its diffused inspiration, its highest vitality, just from
those living traditions that are our greatest inheritance.
We ask for nothing that is foreign to our ideals, rather
we ask for a restoration of those rights, the rights that
are the immortal treasures. We ask only that we may
be given the chance to develop our body and spirit and
mind in that evolution that will re-establish for you ideal
womanhood, not an impossible womanhood such as
poets may dream of, but an ideal womanhood that will
make noble wives who are helpmates, strong mothers,
brave mothers teaching their sons their first lesson of
national service.

Hindu–Muslim Unity

At a public meeting held at Patna on Saturday, 13 October 1917, under the auspices of the Patna City Students' Association, Sarojini Naidu delivered a lecture on Hindu–Muslim Unity. There was a large gathering of both Hindus and Muhammadans. The Hon'ble Rai Bahadur Krishna Sahay was in the chair. After the chairman said a few words about the lecturer, Sarojini Naidu delivered the following speech:

Mr. President and Brothers, Hindus and Mussalmans—I feel today a peculiar sense of responsibility such as I have never felt before when dealing with a subject so intimately bound up with my life strings that I almost hesitate in trying to find words that might be wise enough to suit this occasion in this province at this juncture. When I arrived here a few moments ago, it seemed to me, as I mounted this platform so close to the sacred river flowing beneath, that I got the keynote of what should be my message to you today. (Applause). Centuries ago, when the first Islamic army came to India, they pitched their caravans on the banks of the sacred Ganges and tempered and cooled their swords in the sacred waters. It

131

was the baptism of the Ganges that gave the first welcome to the Islamic invaders that became the children of India as generations went by. And today, in speaking of the Hindu-Moslem Unity, we should bear in mind that historic circumstance, that historic culture, that historic evolution for which the Gangetic valley has stood in bringing about the Hindu-Muslim relationship age after age, and so I trust you will pardon me if I fail, out of my own limited powers, to define the conditions that today might strain your hearts, I seek inspiration from that river which has stood always to the Hindus as the spiritual life that gives wisdom in this life and absolution after death (applause). Today we are confronted with a very critical moment in our national history—what might be and what I trust is merely a passing episode. But it appears to our mind to have assumed a significance that is too great for the people concerned with the future of India to feel lightly about and to permit it to be misconstrued and misrepresented as to cause a cleavage between the two communities. Gentlemen, it is perhaps very indiscreet for a mere stranger like me within this province to speak of difficulties, momentary difficulties, that are peculiarly local; and yet the day has come within our history when nothing that happens to disturb the tranquillity and harmony between the two races can be called local, because there is no province whose life is separated from the life (applause) and suffering of any other part of India. Therefore, you will permit me to consider myself for the moment while I am the guest within this city as one of yourselves. I wish to invoke in your hearts the sense of anxiety, a sense of responsibility that nothing should come to disturb the future harmony of Bihar, the fair progress of the Bihari people, who have always stood for peace and goodwill in the past and whose united hearts should not be cut asunder. It used to be the boast of Bihar that there was no Hindu-Muslim problem in this province and I have heard over and over again of tributes paid by the leaders of other provinces, saying that when the national sky was overcast with doubt and despair, Bihar stood kindling the torch of love and union. There was no Hindu-Muslim problem, but only the shining prescience of a hopeful unity that was real and not merely born of any political exigencies. Then, shall we for the moment allow that fair record to be stained? Shall we because ignorance brings cleavage, let that record be stained to bitterness among those who should know better, who should think better to confound that all differences are merely temporary illusions, that the reality cannot be broken, and that where knowledge comes the understanding of love must also come? It is only because we are ignorant that we are divided and it is the sacred mission of enlightenment to bring not the lesson of quarrel but the lesson of peace (shouts of h*ear hear*). That is the problem with which we have to deal today. For what is the Hindu-Muslim Unity? We hear it spoken of vigorously, we hear it spoken of unceasingly, we hear it spoken of passionately. But we have defined to ourselves its practical issues? What is the meaning, what is the significance of the Hindu-Moslem Unity? There is so much misconception abroad that, if a Muslim shows sympathy towards a Hindu, he becomes a traitor and that if a Hindu shows sympathy towards a Mussalman, he becomes an outcaste. But what is the reason of this mistrust of those who stand as links between the two races? Nothing save our misreading of the entire purpose of national history. The problem of the Hindu-Muslim Unity stands like this: there are in India two communities (I will not say two races), two communities that are separated by what they consider the difference of creeds. But when you come to analyze this difference of creed, you begin to find that after all, fundamentally, the teaching that came in the wake of the Muslim conquerors was the same as the teaching that arose in the great hymns in the sacred mountain regions of the Himalayas and on the sacred Ganges five thousand years ago. It means essentially the love of truth, the love of purity, the service of humanity, the search for wisdom, the great lessons of self-sacrifice, the worship of the same transcendent Spirit, no matter whether in one language it was called Allah and in another Parameshwar (applause). After all, what is this antagonism between creed and creed? Antagonism is merely the asset of the ignorant. They are not the weapons of the wise (hear hear} who realize that after all it is only the misunderstanding of the essential truth wherein lies the difficulty in launching across that golden bridge of sympathy that brings together the two great communities whose fundamental teaching is the love of God and the service of men. And then in this great country the Moslems came to make their home not to carry spoils and to go back to their own home but to build permanently here their home and create a new generation for the enrichment of the Motherland. How can they live separate from the people of the soil? Does history say that in the past they have so lived separate? Or rather it says that once having chosen to take up their abode in this land, they became the children of the soil, the very flesh of our flesh and blood of our blood. Gentlemen, history has said that the foreign emperors sought not to divide and rule, but to unite the people and so build an imperishable guarantee of their own power and administration (loud cheers). It may not be strange to you when you look back and see what were the chief characteristics of the Mughal rule. Not that the Hindus were kept at arms' length, but that the Emperor Akbar took his son to Rajputana so that the blood of the conqueror and the blood of the conquered were mixed to create a new generation of Indians in India. That was the marital union between the Mussalmans and the Hindus.

Do not for a moment misunderstand this. I have quoted this symbolically as typical of what should be the kinship between the two great communities in this land. Keep your separate entities, keep your separate creed, but bring to the federated India the culture of centuries to enrich with all those contributions that each has to make for the sum total, for the healthful growth of the national progress. Who says that we want an Indian marriage between the Hindus and the Mussalmans so that each might lose its own special characteristics? India is so complex in the problems of her civilization, in her races and her creeds that it is impossible, that it is even very undesirable—nay, psychologically false—were we to say that we desire a unity that means the merging of the separate races to make one kind of common life for the common weal of the country. What we want is this: that for the evolution of national life we want the Mussalmans to bring their special characteristics and so we want the Hindus to contribute theirs and considering the chivalry of the past allow no minority to suffer. We are not limiting ourselves to the contributions of the Hindu-Muslim culture alone, but we want the special contributions which the Zoroastrians and the Christians and other races scattered over this land can bring us. Gentlemen, do not for a moment entertain any idea of exclusion, harbour any thought of isolation of one group from another, of one sect from another. But let each bring its own quota of special contributions as free gifts offered lovingly and generously. At the feet of the great Motherland, for the swelling of the national Commonwealth. What is the special contribution of the Mussalmans? And what is the special contribution of the Hindus? We have only to go back and look to their own records, their own annals, their own culture. The Hindus have to bring to modern evolution of life the principal qualities of that spiritual civilization that gave to the world not merely the tone of the Upanishads, but created for the intellectual and the illiterate alike such glorious types of virtue, courage, wisdom, truth, as Kama among men and Savitri among women, that most genius of the Hindus, that spiritual passion, that fervour of self-abnegation, the great first realization that the true measure of life is not the material, not the temporal, but the spiritual—that is the special contribution that the Hindu race has to make to the future evolution of India. And what of the Mussalmans? The first of the great world religions that thirteen hundred years ago laid down the first fundamental principles of Democracy was the religion of Islam. In the twentieth century, we hear that the ideal of the future is Democracy. In the West, they speak of it as if it was a thing new-born, the discovery of the western people, but the first secret of this great world-wide Democracy was laid in the desert sands of Arabia by a dreamer of the desert and it is the peculiar privilege of this spiritual children to bring to this mystic India of spiritual value that human sense of Democracy that makes the king and the beggar equal (Applause). Now it is this principle of Democracy that implies certain mental qualities that is inseparable from Democracy. It implies a certain inviolable sense of justice that gives to every man his equal chance in the evolution of national life and these we want imported into our national life, assimilated into our national life, which the Hindu community cannot with its system of exclusion that has been the misinterpreted characteristic of a system that made it merely a true division of responsibility. I say the Hindu community by itself cannot evolve it because,

Hindu as I am, I stand here to confess the limitation of my community. We have not mastered the fundamental equality that is the privilege of Islam. What is mutual co-operation? What is the meaning of unity? Not merely bringing together the separate qualities, the mystic genius of the Hindus (loud cries of hear hear) and the dynamic forces of Islam. We go further, we want that from the very beginning of our childhood there should be an interchange of culture. We want that Mussalmans should hear from their nurses the great history, the great legends that are the inspiration of every man and woman; and we want that the Hindu children sitting in the twilight by the peepal tree should thrill with the history, the chivalry of the Arabian armies that carried in one hand the torch of knowledge and in the other, the sword of their own conviction. It is by this interchange of knowledge and culture of each community from its babyhood that we shall be able to build up not merely that kinship that is born of political expediency.

Politics are sordid, politics are vulgar. They deal with current problems which are important today and forgotten tomorrow. Politics deals with current details. Nationality deals with the character of the nation and the character of the Indian people is such a complex thing that you cannot in one little phrase say that it is Aryan. You can only say that the character of the Indian is the achievement neither of the mystic qualities of the Aryan race nor of the dynamic qualities of the Semitic people alone, but the union of the power that thinks and the courage that acts, the mixture of dream and action which alone can make for the true uplifting of the national life. Now I have come to the essential point. It used to be said with reference to Italian liberty, that Mazzini by himself was merely a dreamer and that Garibaldi by himself was merely a soldier and that either of them individually could not have built what is the great liberated Italy of today. But it was the genius of Mazzini, the dreamer, that became the deed of Garibaldi that made Italy free. And so in the evolution of our national history the Hindus are the Mazzini and the Mussalmans the Garibaldi. A combination of the visionary, the dreamer with the statesman, the soldier, the mystic genius with the virility of manhood—that is what we want today in this great India of ours. Then, when we set out to reach this high goal to unite, the consecrated fire that unities the different aspirations of the two different communities, of dream and actuality, shall we pause by the way, because of a little quarrel here, a little faction there? Shall we be deterred from this triumph of a self-realization of a united people simply on account of some personal resentment here, some passing grudge there, or shall we push on? We have before us only a few difficulties and the goal is so radiant that we cannot stop by the way, for the way is long and our life is short and we cannot pass into the shadows of generations that have gone behind, leaving their works unfinished and incomplete. Therefore, we cannot loiter by the wayside in settling personal quarrels.

We can only set our faces forward. There is a work for
the united army to do, There is no separate act for us, no
separate gain or loss, no separate sufferings, no separate
failure, no separate victory, but one common march, one
common suffering, one common starvation, one common
affinity which death alone can sever (prolonged cheers).

Gentlemen, these words sound, you will say, like
the words of a Hindu visionary, but believe me that the
words of visionaries are always the inmost thought that
is common in the heart of a nation. There is no poet who
has sung, there is no prophet who has spoken in the past
except that he was the articulate voice of the people that
had not yet found words to suit their aspirations. Because,
after all, when you come to consider all that makes the
art of a nation, the philosophy of a nation, the literature
of a nation, the achievement of a nation, why do you
honour the maker of the music, the sculptor, the builder
of those temples? Because these are the embodiments
of the common vision, the common aspiration, the
common experience of unity, and so, no man is separate
from another and when the voice of a prophet speaks,
calling like the trumpet, it is only that focussed music
of the Indian people and his race that speaks in hymns
and everyday life. When I stand up and say to you, let
there be this union between vision and action, it is simply
that I am articulating your inmost desires and giving
words to our inmost conviction. So your leaders are the
embodiments of your own dreams and desires, of your
own capacity and energies and when you stoop to blame

your leaders that they are not true, when you say they are not worthy, they are not able, have you realized what a condemnation of yourselves it is that you are not worthy enough yourselves as followers to evolve worthy and great leaders who are true to their cause?

Gentlemen, when I hear men say we have no leaders, I say, is it because India has no men? Remember that the law of demand and supply always holds good in all things alike small and great and it is only by the worth of your leaders that the worth of followers of people can be gauged, because, as I said, no man is an original thinker amongst us. Every one of us is but the mirror of his own desires, the embodiments, the images of his own souls and aspirations. Therefore, I pray, consider your shares in co-operating to bring about that reality of your dreams for which you are ready to suffer. I trust you are ready to suffer, and in what way shall these things be done? The way is so simple that when it is put to you in terms of daily life, the glamour, no doubt, becomes less dazzling in your daily action, when you hear it said in the advertisement of lectures on the Hindu-Muslim Unity. That is a magnificent phrase but in daily action, what does it mean? It means the simple fact that you love your neighbour as yourselves, you realize his humanity as common with your experiences and aspirations of life, his failures, his triumph, his hopes and fears, his culture and ignorance which are the common inheritance between you and him (cheers). There is no difference (hear, hear). because of your common aspirations, your common destiny of humanity.

It becomes a very simple thing to say that all men are neighbours of one another, brothers, blood ties, because they have the same tears and the same laughter. Therefore, perhaps, they may have the same kind of aspirations; the same quality of men may have the same kind of aspirations; so why make difference between the tillers of the soil whether he is a Muslim or a Hindu? Does he not suffer from drought, from the failure of harvest, from pestilence from locusts? The schoolmaster, whether he be a Hindu or a Mussalman, has he not the same responsibility of creating within his hands (is he not a sharer of a common responsibility, I ask) a bond between brother and brother whether he be a Hindu or a Mussalman? Then, when floods come, and famines come, and plagues come, do not all of us suffer equally? Why make difference between men? Are there different angels of death for the Hindus and Mussalmans to carry them off? Does not every man feel that he must co-operate with each other, what matters if he be a Hindu or a Mussalman? Shall not a Brahman carry on his head the corpse of a Mussalman and shall not a Sayyid carry on his head the corpse of a Hindu? What has the corpse of a Hindu or a Mussalman done not to deserve the same sense of honour from each of us who are equally created by God and who are equally subject to mortality? These are trivial details of life. And when, gentlemen, feelings run high and passions are roused and when men forget this common brotherhood, what are the duties of those whose visions are not obscured? What are the duties of those who have not been excited by some little trifling cause that has such awful, far-reaching effect? Remember that blessed is the man that makes peace and thrice cursed is the man or woman that sets a little spark of fire into flames. Is not that what we have to remember when we see two brothers fighting at the street corner? Shall not we go to them and say 'Cease, brothers, be friends.' That is the symbolism of what we should do when two communities are at the parting way of national life. Cursed be every man and woman of every rank and creed in this great country that incites, that excites instead of quelling, that urges on instead of quenching, that separates instead of uniting, that, gentlemen, brings up the differences between creed and creed instead of preaching that fundamental truth of humanity, the humanity of one God, the one Indivisible in all men. That is the meaning of the Hindu–Muslim Unity—not resentment, not suspicion, not the ungenerous schism that divides and says aggressively we are a majority and you are a minority and so shall trample on you. These things, gentlemen, are the cancers in the growth of social life. Rather we want the chivalry of the majority—the original children of this land to say to their Muslim brothers, 'Take what we have because there is no division between you and us. Are we not the children of the common Motherland and shall the elder, by the priority of his older age, wrest from you your equal inheritance?' This is the feeling of a generous love, of brotherly love that we want to establish as a thing flawless, and in the hearts of the Hindus towards Mussalmans. We

want to establish that nobility that knows how to trust
without reservation, we want the manliness, the virility
of the soldier that says—you give your word of honour
and that word shall be as a bond of strength, of manhood
that does not consider petty differences of castes and
creeds. Gentleman, that is Hindu-Muslim Unity. Not the
betraying of one community by its own leaders against
another, not the selling of the community for the sake of
the honour that might come but rather the responsible
sense of co-operation in the mutual reverence for each
other's creed, mutual love for each other's civilization,
mutual trust in your common good intention and co-
operation and equal responsibilities in the evolution of
your great national life of tomorrow. That is the meaning
of the Hindu-Muslim Unity.

Once more we turn to the sacred river flowing
beneath us; what has been the symbolism of that river
through the centuries? What has been the symbolism of
that river? What is the symbolism, I say, that age after age
has made it sacred not merely in Sanskrit but in Persian
verses as well, that flows giving gift to the land, that
waters the fields of both the Hindu and Mussalman alike.
It has been the inspiration of the Hindu and Mussalman
geniuses as well. The sacred water of this sacred river,
with the solemn music flowing through city after city
has washed away sins after sins of the Hindu people
and has given cold waters to the thirsting armies of the
Mussalmans. And when the great river arrives where it
meets another river, in sacred Prayag, there is the union

with mystic music, soul to soul and heart to heart, of the two great rivers, the Ganga and the Jumna—a Sangam of two rivers each without losing its own characteristics and qualities. And yet it is a perfect union. And that should be the symbol of the Hindu and Muslim Unity, each keeping its own culture, its own individual characteristics, its own purity, its own special colour of its own waters, the music of its own deed even at that point of Union. That is the meaning of the Sangam of national life. That is, gentlemen, the true meaning of the Hindu-Muslim Unity. I will not detain you longer because I have another function to attend—something, gentlemen, which does not a little to contribute towards this Unity.

I speak of children studying each the culture of the other that makes for mutual unity; but there is another thing that, translated into national life, is sure to bind the children of the two communities in a common bond. That other act is the unifying influence of sports that teach us fairplay, justice, co-operation, harmony, equal competition and therefore train us in all those qualities that are needed for virile manhood—the eye, the brain, the mind, the arm, and, above all things, that training and discipline which will evolve our manhood of tomorrow. That also makes for the Hindu-Muslim Union. And now when I have given you the message of the river, the symbol of the river, the symbol of its Union, symbols that you should enshrine in your hearts I will ask your leave to go and give away the shield that stands also in its own important manner as the reality of Hindu-Muslim Unity (prolonged and enthusiastic cheers).

The Congress-League Scheme

Sarojini Naidu, in seconding the Resolution on the Congress-League Scheme of Reforms at the Madras Special Provincial Conference on 21 December 1917, said:

Mr. President, ladies, and gentlemen of the Madras Presidency, I do not know exactly what right I have to stand in a Special Conference of the Madras Presidency to address you on so momentous a question as has been embodied in this resolution. But as the time has long since gone by when anything could remain merely provincial, when any question could remain merely local, I crave your indulgence for a few moments to add my words of support to this resolution.

What are the strongest arguments that one can bring in favour of the irreducible minimum of demands for reform? Last September, I spent the entire season when the Imperial Legislative Council was in session, and day after day, sitting in the visitors' gallery; my heart grew bitter within me for this reason. Some of the most important and vital questions that would conduce to the progress of Indians as Indians were brought up and as resolution after resolution was brought up in favour of simultaneous examinations for the Civil Service, or the proportion of the recruits to the Civil Service, or the amelioration of the condition of the railway passengers or anything that might help a little to remove the political or the social defects of the nation, what did I find but an instinctive and invincible combination of the official and non-official European element in permanent opposition against every resolution? (*Cries of shame, shame*). That is what I said to a friend of the Secretary of State who is with him that after all our demands are based not on a political grievance so much but because our national self-respect has been trampled. It is not, as I said, a question of four-fifths elected or one-fifth nominated, not a question of so many more portfolios for Indians and so many less for Europeans. It is rather the fundamental question of our national self-respect being restored and that is the origin of this irreducible minimum of this Congress-League scheme of reforms (cheers).

A few months ago, I was present in Delhi when the great field of discussion came in the budget. The budget had been prepared, it had been passed, published and then by a farce—that is an insult—the Indian members were allowed to give their opinion on the budget. It is, as my friend Mr. Jinnah said, to put the cart before the horse, to pass the budget and invite discussion afterwards (cheers). Now, if we Indians have the control over the finances of our country, it cannot be that important estimates are passed for the current year, the money is disbursed or ear-marked for any department without the sanction of the Indian members who have at heart the interests of the country. Then, if you want more representation, representation that is not merely nominal but real and that those who represent the people in the Council of the Viceroy should be true spokesmen of the people, we must have our control over the revenues and the taxes because we alone know what presses hard on our people (cheers). We must have the power to control the educational policies because we see around us those deadening results of foreign policy of education in which our voice has not been heard. Therefore, more vital than anything is it that the educational portfolio should be in the hands of the Indian Member of Council. When we have a large number of Indians represented in the Council, the voice of the many cannot be denied and when the voice of the many is heard, then that one crucial reason of our deterioration, that is the right to avenge and the right to defend our country, that inalienable right of man of being able to protect his household, will come to us.

With regard to communal representation, I personally am quite in agreement with Mr. K.P. Raman Menon and Mr. P. Kesava Pillai. And I think you will find that the majority of thinking men, Hindus and Muslims, are in agreement that the principle of communal representation is not the ideal one, but in practical politics sometimes we have to go by expediency towards the path of the ideal and that is why till we are able to establish that abiding trust in each other, love and co-operation, there should

be communal representation. It is a temporary barrier
between community and community and directly trust is
established, Mussalmans will say, 'Oh Brethren Hindus,
we trust you.' The non-Brahman will say, 'Oh subtle
Brahmans we trust you.' The Panchamas, who carry the
bond of centuries, will say, 'Oh Castemen, we trust you.'
Nobody will want separate representation but we will
establish the true democracy of Indian life by seeing that
the best men shall represent the best interests of India.
Now, over this question of Muslim representation, a lot
has been written and said for and against. My own feeling
is this—and I see a Mussalman friend looking at me very
critically—(cheers) that had you not provided generously
for the separate representation, it were not possible that
within five years Mussalman brethren would have stood
shoulder to shoulder with you, for, disorganized and so
much behind the Hindu community they were. Because
they began their political education later, it was necessary
for them to consolidate themselves as a unit first before
they could come in a body to work side by side with their
Hindu brethren. The other day I was speaking to a great
man, a Member of Parliament. He said to me, 'It is all
very well when you talk of Home Rule and the Congress-
League scheme of reforms as the first instalment of Home
Rule. Then, how are you going to make the masses
understand the meaning of Home Rule?' I said, 'As long
as we are patriotic in English, we cannot make the masses
understood. But we are having our vernacular patriotism
just now. There are groups of men who have made it

possible to have Mr. Gandhi's monster petition signed
by the same masses.' He said, 'But how do you explain
Home Rule to them?' I said, 'We can always explain
the view by explaining to them their past. One has only
to say to the villager that this Home Rule is no more
than an expansion of his village councils and his own
village democracies. It is the modern interpretation of his
village panchayat liberated, enriched and co-ordinated
to a vast central focus of power.' But I said to him that
there was one new element in it that did not belong to
ancient India and that is I take a little trouble to adjust
the views of the ordinary peasant in India and especially
in Southern India. In Northern India where the Hindu
and the Muslim have worked and lived side by side, it
is no novel idea. But in the South where the problem
is not so vivid, so urgent and frequent, it is not always
possible to make the Hindu villager understand that
principle of the Home Rule democracy. But I said to him,
'It is nothing that is difficult, nothing stands in our way
because the heart of literate India beats in unison with the
heart of the illiterate India and they will not be left out in
any scheme of reform because without them we cannot
work. They are the fates that will carry us to the goal.' He
was struck by what I said, but he said: 'That is all right
about the masses. But what about the Mussalmans?' I
said, 'This Congress-League scheme is the work of the
flower of the Hindu and Mahomedan intellect and spirit,
combined representatives and elected people of the
two communities have framed this. Where there is no

education, there is unity; where there is education, there
is unity but where there is half education amenable to
persuasion and coercion, there is no unity.' (cheers) So,
gentlemen, we must support the Congress-League scheme.
It is true it is an imperfect scheme. All schemes when you
bring them to the merciless test of logic are illogical. And
who is there from the Viceroy downward that is going to
suggest a better scheme? If there is a better scheme less
illogical and more perfect, we are willing to put it before
the people and let them try the comparative merits of the
schemes. We are not so rigid and hidebound in our own
prejudices and predilections that we must enforce our
own wishes in the best interests of the people as against
better schemes. We are not so illogical ourselves, though
our schemes may be. You can support the Congress-
League scheme, not merely by raising your hand and
by offering your vote but in your own by carrying out
the principles of this scheme, demanding and fulfilling
the demands in your own community and insisting that
the education policy of your own horizon is within your
own hands. Begin to take a little more interest in matters
around you. Do not put by your patriotic instincts for
times and seasons convenient to you. It does not mean
that all of you should be politicians but it does mean that
all of you should be patriots. Patriotism is not a thing
divorced from real life. It is the flame that burns within
the soul, a gem-like flame that cannot be extinguished.
The Congress-League scheme is a little thing. If you be
not united and earnest, even that little is too much of a

burden for you to sustain, but if you are united, if you forget your community and think of the nation, if you forget your city and think of the province, if you forget you are a Hindu and remember the Mussalman, if you forget you are a Brahman and remember the Panchama, then and then alone will India progress (loud cheers and applause).

Co-operation Among Communities

At the First Annual Conference of the Madras Presidency Association on 22 December 1917, in moving a Resolution on the above subject, Mrs Sarojini Naidu said:

Mr. President and Members of the Madras Presidency Association, it sometimes happens that when one's thoughts and energies have become concentrated in and consecrated to one single purpose, in course of time one's name becomes associated with a certain cause, one's name becomes identified with a certain purpose. And today if I have been honoured, I, a mere stranger in Madras, with the proposal of a resolution, which, in my opinion, is the most vital resolution of this Conference, it is because in my humble way I have always sought for that unity which this resolution seeks to embody (cheers). The resolution runs thus—

That this Conference would appeal to the various communities of South India to sink their local differences in this supreme moment in the history of India and sincerely co-operate with one another for the general uplift of the Motherland.

It is very curious that last evening, when I went home from the Special Provincial Conference, I found a letter awaiting me which was meant to reach me in time before I came to the Special Conference. It was not from any section of the Hindu community at all, but it was from a community of Southern India. It contained an appeal to me as a friend of every community, whether in the South or in the North, to use my influence—if I should have any—to use my persuasion—if I should have the power to persuade—for greater co-operation among us all just at this moment. I might ask the great Hindu community of the South, in the name of my Mussalman brethren, to build up this unity of which we all speak, on a real brotherly basis of give and take. The day before yesterday I was present at the meeting of the Muslim League and it was my great privilege to be allowed to speak there on the same great question, the one question on which I am able to speak. I spoke to them adequately in your name. I asked my Mussalman brethren of the South to learn the brotherly task of give and take, always to work in harmony, in co-operation, without resentment.

I pointed out to them that had the Hindu community not been brotherly, the division of loaves and fishes that have yet to come would not have been so generous. Today I should stand as an ambassador of the great Mussalman community and ask in their name before I begin my proper task of supporting the resolution, that if you are sincere in wishing to pass this resolution, of sinking differences and of bringing about co-operation and harmony into your lives, you will start not with smaller divisions but first learn to heal the big cleavage that still exists today between the two great races, between the two great faiths. As a friend of the Mussalmans [I] would ask my brother Hindu, not to raise any objection if the Mussalmans who respect our feelings, ask that the Hindus should respect their feelings. There is sympathy. They want you to prove that you are truly brotherly. If you truly wish India to be united and not divided, even as you value your religious beliefs, even as you cherish your religious faiths and your prejudices, if they ask that as a token of the gift of your love, you will not object to the little thing they demand that when our Hindu processions pass the Moslem mosques, they shall not violate one of the primary mandates of Islam, that there should not be sound to break the silence of the mosque. It seems to me that the existence of an Association like this presupposes not a show of a wide division between the two races and the two creeds, a sharp bitter division originally but now happily by patriotic love grown narrower and narrower, a division between the children of the same race, the sons of the same race, only a little divided by one having the birthright of spirit and the other the birthright of material things. Both in the speech of the Chairman of the Reception Committee and the speech of your President today, we find that though the Madras Presidency Association was started as a sort of speaker of the non-Brahman community, though it was founded as a channel of the expression of the community of non-

Brahmans determined to have a responsible voice in the shaping of the national destiny, they have been able by their patriotism to rise above their own patty personal needs and desires. 'This is a supreme moment in our history,' says the text of the resolution. It is a supreme moment in our history, because today we Indians not only of the South, but the Indians of the united India are asking for that which is the birthright of every civilized nation. We are asking for the right to live within our own land. We are the children of the soil whose flesh is made out of the clays and waters of India, whose spirits have been kindled by the eternal stars of India, we are asking for a right not to be exiles in our own land (cheers). But unless that cry of the exiled children of the Mother goes forth as one voice of many million chords, one indivisible voice of many million chords, rising out of one undivided, indivisible heart of India, how dare we say, 'Give us freedom because we are united.' I have been told on good authority which I cannot divulge that the great Viceroy, in the course of these few weeks when India has been knocking at his doors, has never been so puzzled as in this historic city because the heart is divided here. One little rift might make him say that the music of unity is not perfect. I ask you, friends in the South of India, to remember the great traditions of your great province. They say today in the North—and I have heard it over and over again with pride because remember that you have adopted me, by marriage I belong to you—'Is it to the South that we must turn for inspiration, to that South which we for years and years looked at as something apart, alone, asleep, unrelated to the manifold progress of which we are proud? Yes, it is true today. I think the lamp burns very brightly in the Soul of yours with a flame that sheds lustre far and reaches even the historic North. But where that historic North has already achieved unity, the bitter antagonisms and animosities which filled the North have come through the crucible of many centuries of hate into a period of harmony and peace, here in the South, where the lamp burns brightly, the house is divided against itself. How great the dissolution and how great the despair? No despair is so deadly as the despair of an injured faith. If you to whom the eyes of the rest of India are turned today hurt that faith in your unity, that faith in your power, you have done wrong not to yourselves alone but to the cause of the Indian Unity which you should embody and inspire (cheers), I ask you, therefore, without entering into details that are technical, without elaborating about representations and proportions, to consider the ideal that I would hold out before you, the ideal of co-operation.

Why should there be division between caste and caste? What was the meaning, the purpose, the significance, and the power of the caste division in the old days? What was it but a division of labour for the glory of the Motherland, so that each within his own sphere could contribute perfect service that should enrich the wide diversity of life? It was to build up, to create and foster national culture and national consciousness. Was that great system subtly built of a knowledge of human functions and possibilities meant to bring division? Were the law makers enemies of their Motherland that they brought about this division of sects and castes? No. It was built up so that India might be served, each community honouring itself and finding its perfect expression through some service which would be best suited to its own way of thought, to its own capacity of achievement, its own sources of inspiration, and its own opportunity of realisation. Have we grown so civilized that we have become untrue to our own social, intellectual, and spiritual principles? (Cheers). Have we become so alienated from the inner meanings of our evolution that what was meant to be a source of richer unity has become today a source of disunion, disintegration, degradation that affected the honour and progress of the Motherland? You have all made separate demands for reform, Brahmans, non-Brahmans, Mussalmans, and Panchamas have gone on deputations. But what good are all these deputations, all these divided attempts? Let there be a hundred thousand deputations. If they can go in one united spirit with their different forms of expression of the cause, then each fresh demand freshly reiterated would mean the emphasizing of the same demand. Today we stand so that if the Angels of Heaven would sit in judgment, as to the real meaning and link between demand and demand, very different in fact, he might be puzzled to know what was just and what was unjust. But we need not call the Angels of Heaven, nor need we await the leisure of another nation for justice (cheers). Justice is within the soul of a nation, justice is the treasure of a nation, justice is the honour of a nation. If a nation chooses to rob itself, to dishonour itself, to be untrue to itself, not the Angels of Heaven, not the ministers of the King shall stay it. But if a nation chooses to honour itself, fulfil its duty and rise to the height of its own ambition, what prevents it but its own desires, what prevents it but its own folly, what prevents it but its own personal animosities and personal cleavages? I ask you, children of the immortal South, during the forthcoming years to be true to yourself, just to yourself, sink all divisions, obliterate all differences, forget all feuds, annihilate all hatreds, become one in the service of the Motherland, for, as I said, your flesh, Brahman or non-Brahman, is made out of the clays and waters of the South and your spirit is filled by the breath of Her who is Bharata Mata.

Self-Government for India: Speech at the Calcutta Congress

In supporting the Resolution on Self-Government at the Calcutta Congress in December 1917, Mrs Sarojini Naidu said:

Several years ago, in this historic city, the modern nation builder, Dadabhai Naoroji, proclaimed the immortal message of Swaraj in your ears. I do not think that there was one single heart amongst you that did not respond to the call of your birthright that had so long been withheld from you. We are gathered here today to vindicate the message that he then gave, to confirm the truth that he proclaimed, and we demand the fulfilment of the dream that he dreamt for you on that memorable occasion. If I stand before you as a chosen representative of united India, it is only because the womanhood of the nation stands by you today and you require no proof more worthy, more convincing of your evidence for responsible and complete Self-Government than the sense of instinctive and fundamental justice you show in letting the voice of Indian womanhood speak and confirm the vision, the demand, the endeavour, the ambition of Indian manhood.

Other speakers having spoken before me and explained to you in detail the scheme that you have propounded, the ambition that the scheme embodied and the aspiration that you are at the point of achieving, I shall only strive to interpret something that goes beyond the details of that scheme and that is the ideal that has been represented in this resolution. Remember, whatever may be the details of the proposition, whatever may be the facts and factors of any practical politics that you contemplate, its permanent inspiration is the spirit in which these demands and these aspirations are conceived and fulfilled today. What is it that we demand? Nothing new, nothing startling, but a thing that is as old as life, as old as human consciousness, and that is the birthright of every soul in this world. Remember that within your own province, within your own territories, you should have a living chance and not be disinherited as exiles in your own land, slaves in your own territories, dumb to all things, blind to all things, deaf to all things that other nations are enjoying. That day is over when we were content to be slaves in bondage, intellectual, and political, because the day of division is over. No race can be separated from another race in this great land. There is no longer an India of the Hindu or an India of the Mussalman, but it is an India which is a united India. Arguments are brought forward, you all know how cleverly and subtly, that India has always been a conquered country, a country always under foreign political domination. It is true, but India, you should know, is a great country with 5,000 years of

Vedic culture that absorbed and enriched itself within the Aryan culture, Buddhist culture, and European culture of the world. What is really at the base of all our grievances is that our self-respect has been trodden to dust, that our manhood has been challenged, that the primary right of man to defend his honour, to defend his women and to protect his country, has been taken away from him. That is the deadliest insult that has not merely emasculated and embittered but has almost slain beyond redemption the spirit of the heroic Indian. Not that you have lost political power and domination, but that you have lost the spirit within you that was your birthright and inviolable treasure. You say that the Moghuls were your rulers. What was the policy of the Moghul rulers? They became part and parcel of the Indian race. They gave to the Indian people those rights and responsibilities which we demand today from the British Throne. These things which are embodied in the scheme for responsible autonomy were given to the Indians. In the time of Akbar's rule, the power of the purse belonged to the conquered people of that Moghul Emperor. Did that power lead to differences? Did it breed disloyalty? No, that power knit together the peoples so alien to one another in race, faith, tradition, and culture. With what result? So, far from impoverishing the intellectual cultures of India, the foreign conquests succeeded in assimilating foreign cultures with ours and the valour of the Children of the Sword has added to the valour of the Children of the Sun. In that combination India was honoured. India had not to face the question of submission and implied bondage to conquerors. When we talk of Responsible Government, it does not mean an illusion of power. Power without responsibility is demoralizing. We demand not license of power, but we demand all the dignity, the sanity, the creative authority of power that is responsible to itself and responsible to the nation. We do not want to be separated from the life of the people. We want no divided power. Our goal is the same, but temperaments are different, conditions are different, environments are different, and all these things being considered, India is not an India of one race or another, of one party or another, of the Moderate or the Extremist; but in politics the ideal is always there, but there must be a certain amount of expediency used. That is the only compromise that has been made. All life is a life of compromises. The only thing that matters is that for the sake of the weaker the stronger must be prepared to make some sacrifices. Who says that there is a man or woman here today who does not desire, waking or sleeping, that does not dream that autonomy, that freedom, that liberty, that is self-contained and conveyed by this resolution? One community has got into the race earlier than another community, and possesses advantage by that circumstance and that is the meaning of the compromise that we feel for the weaker. We confess that it is a compromise, but we say that the demand that we make in the Congress-League Scheme is an irreducible minimum and that minimum should not be delayed one hour longer. I am only a woman and I should like to say to you all, when your hour strikes, when you need torch-bearers in the darkness to lead you, when you want standard-bearers to uphold your banner and when you die for want of faith, the womanhood of India will be with you as the holders of your banner, and the sustainers of your strength. And if you die, remember, the spirit of Padmini of Chitor, is enshrined with the manhood of India (loud cheers).

A Vision of India's Future Women

The following speech was delivered by Sarojini Naidu on the occasion of the prize distribution at the Kanya Maha Vidyalaya, Jullundur, on 31 March 1918:

My Punjabi Friends, you have all seen in your cities, it is a very common sight in India, the wandering singer with a stick on his shoulder with two bundles tied on its each end going from city to city singing his songs. I stand before you today as a wandering singer like that with all my possessions carried in my two bundles—one a little bundle of dreams and another a growing bundle of hopes. These are the only two things which I have in this world.

Exactly like a wandering singer I, too, am going from city to city and like him, too, I have always something to dream about every new city that I visit. My dreams have not always proved shattered illusions but they have come some time as realized hopes too. Today we in India stand upon the verge of destiny, a glorious destiny (cheers). This is no mere nightmare, no mere poet's dream, but the dawn is already in sight, the glorious dawn that would light up the eastern sky and fill it with light (loud cheers).

Every province, every part of India, has its own peculiar characteristics, symbols you may call them, the promise of what the dawn is to bring and my little dreams are clustered round these symbols and promise. When I think of the great Maharashtra, I dream not of the glory of the Peshwas, not of the clashing swords, not of the warring hordes of Shivaji, but I see and think of the Fergusson College of Poona with its noble band of professors working, silently and selflessly, for the educational progress of the Maharashtra. In Madras, I see the little College at Masulipatam with its burning idealism trying to hold up all that is noblest and purest in our national life. In the United Provinces, it is not Benares, the Eternal City, the holy Kasi that I dream of, nor do I dream of the glories of Oadh, the splendour of its rulers that are no more, but I dream of the two streams which like the great Ganges and the Jumna are going to meet and mingle with each other, the two streams from the Aligarh Muslim and the Benares Hindu Universities (cheers).

But what is the dream that I dream here in the Punjab? Not the great military traditions of the province, nor the battles it has fought and won have I dreamt of; my first vision of the Punjab has been this cloister, this sanctuary, this stronghold of the women of the North.

The women of the Punjab who are to be the redemption of this land of the five rivers, greeted me first in the Punjab and I would never forget their kindness and their welcome (cheers).

Eleven years ago, the Principal of this School (cheers) a Saraswati in reality, a little, frail, timid Hindu widow clad in her simple white garb, came on a pilgrimage to my city of Hyderabad. I remember to this day, I vividly and distinctly remember the day when she stood there amidst hundreds of Hindus and Muhammadans, appealing for her school. It was on this occasion eleven years ago, that I delivered my first speech, on the request of my friends to say something. I never dreamt that day that I would come eleven years later to the same school on whose behalf I delivered my maiden speech (cheers).

The most hopeful sign that meets my eye in this institution is the stand that it has taken on national grounds, the roots that it has laid on the soils of the country, taking its inspiration from its past and yet living in the present. Had I said that the school was an ideal one in every respect, I would be paying not a tribute but sounding its death-knell. Imperfections it has, but it is perfect because it is true to the past and yet alive to the modern conditions of life (cheers).

We often hear, not without a taunt, that the education of girls during the last three generations has been a failure. It could not but be so, it would have been strange if it had not been so. It could not be fruitful because it went away from our traditions and ideals. Our educationists are now awake to the fact that education should and can only be on national lines. We have produced exceptional women and brilliant women, too, not because of the present system of education but in spite of it.

If we want to reconstruct our educational system, it must be along a course which would continue to preserve the best traditions of the East and West. Our standard of education of Indian women should be a normal average. Not that one of our women should be pointed out with admiration as a wonderful and a brilliant woman for her culture and attainments, but rather people should point out with horror at an illiterate woman in India.

Only this morning I was reading in one of your daily papers of what Lord Haldane recently said in connection with the granting of voting rights to the women of England. He said that the day is not very distant when people in England would wonder at their refusal to grant the parliamentary rights to women just as they now wonder as to how people kept slaves in the past. I think that time would also soon come to India when we too would wonder as to how we could keep out women in ignorance.

Remember that woman does not merely keep the hearth-fire of your homes burning, but she keeps also the beacon fire of national life aflame. It is she who keeps the soldier-heart in time of battle and the priest-heart at the time of peace (cheers). The power of self-surrender and self-realization had been the typical characteristics of Indian womanhood. This dual capacity of the personal and impersonal in her relation to man had always marked the Indian women. In this institution, too, I find manifest that spirit of self-surrender, joyous self-surrender, and self-realization. These are the qualities that make the

Indian women great and these are the qualities that I am glad to find in this Vidyalaya (loud cheers).

Today, we who dream dreams of the coming women of India have our hopes centred round institutions like this (cheers), institutions like that of Professor Karve at Poona, not the institutions that only slavishly imitate men's college but the institutions that would send forth to the world women not merely brought up and fed in the dry pages of lifeless books but rather women trained in the beauties and necessities of life. These women would go forth not bearing the burden of dead knowledge but culture transmuted in the services of humanity (loud cheers).

The historic significance of this crowd gathered here today lies not in its number for I have addressed crowds five times larger than this; but its significance lies in the presence of the very large number of women that are gathered here. Their presence here is the indication of the coming comradeship between men and women in India. The old partition between Mardana and Zenana is broken down forever. It is in the comradeship of sexes that future India shall come out man and woman working hand in hand and supplementing each other (cheers)

Friends, tomorrow again, I shall fare forth as a singing wanderer with my two bundles of hopes and dreams but never, never shall I forget this institution of yours which is destined to take its legitimate place in the history of the regeneration of India with the promise, the guarantee, almost the realization of the high ideal that it stands for (Loud and prolonged cheers).

Indian Women and the Franchise

Sarojini Naidu moved the following Resolution on Women's Franchise at the eighteenth session of the Bombay Provincial Conference held at Bijapur:

'This Conference welcomes the requisition of the ladies of Bombay inviting the support of this Conference for woman's franchise in India, and places on record its opinion that such a franchise should be given to women but under suitable conditions and recommends that this Resolution be forwarded to the Congress through the Provincial Congress Committee'.

In moving the resolution, Mrs. Naidu said:

I happen to be here to place before you for your unanimous support a most important resolution of this most important Conference. The actual words of the original resolution on which this resolution is based, I need not repeat at this moment, but the sense of it is this: That the Indian women, in this instance the leading women of Bombay, have sent a requisition—in this instance to the Bombay Provincial Conference—asking that the word 'man' should include, politically speaking, 'woman', in discussing the rights of citizenship—in discussing the political rights and franchises, when the Congress-League Scheme comes into existence. Now, with your permission, I would say a word or two as to how this requisition on the part of Indian women came to be placed before the Indian public. Last year the All-India Women's Deputation waited on His Excellency the Viceroy and on Mr. Montagu, and among other things, demanded that women should have their rights politically recognized in the coming Reforms. Well, in the course of the conversation afterwards, that is in the private interview that was granted to some of us, it was the great Mr. Montagu who said to me: 'Do you think that the men of India will allow such a thing, or will they oppose it?' I, feeling that my countrymen were still true to their ancient traditions of chivalry and justice, answered in their name, without hesitation, that so far from objecting to the rights being granted to women, they would support them (cheers). Then, at the All- India Congress Committee's meeting in Calcutta, a resolution demanding a very partial franchise was rather half-heartedly drawn up. It was too partial to please me. But taking the circumstances of the moment into thought I decided that it was not a psychological moment to oppose it. I, therefore, withdrew the resolution, meaning thereby that the women of India should not appeal to the chivalry of the men of India but to their sense of justice. Meanwhile, other women of India by the score—by the hundred—felt awakened to their own responsibilities and to their own privileges in the great reconstruction to come. Their position is this, that so far from demanding the condescension of a partial franchise recommended by men, they are in a position to ask for the full franchise on suitable conditions, whatever the two words may mean. Now, therefore, it is my great privilege to put this resolution before you and to ask you, gentlemen, as responsible citizens, who are demanding large franchises for years, to consider the question of women's franchise from a national point of view. The question is whether in the reconstruction of the national life it will be possible for you to have a rich national life unless and until it is shared and supported by women who are the soul of citizenship and the life of the nation? (Hear, hear). That really is the point at issue. I understand that the conservative instinct of mankind would consider the new doctrine of life or policy a devastating one. But look at Europe, where there is the great tradition of comradeship between the sexes. In India, it is not more than a 'Renaissance'. Those of us who are not so far denationalized as to be ashamed of our past, must realize with thrilling pride how far-reaching was the influence of woman in bringing about political and spiritual unity in ancient India. We are always talking of patriotism in the past and for the future, and we must surely recognize that essence of our ancient traditions which was that the woman was given her rightful place as a responsible comrade and co-sharer with man in the trial of his nation, in the victory of his nation, in the sacrifices of his nation and in upholding the honour and the salvation of his nation (hear, hear). Nowadays, we find that almost every day and almost from every platform resolutions are passed meaning to say: 'We are ready to give the last drop of blood for the salvation of our country,' but when you say this, you must remember that you are only a part-possessor, only a co- trustee of that life-blood that you are ready to offer. When you are ready to have the citizen army, when you are ready to send your sons for the defence of the Empire, when you are ready to stake your life and your wealth and all that you hold dear for the freedom of India, you should remember that you are accepting half the responsibilities for India's future in trust. When the Spartan soldier went to fight, it was his mother who said to him, 'Come back victorious or touch the shield.' Remember that in all great national crises, it is the man that goes out, but it is the woman's hope and woman's prayer that nerves him—nerves his arm to become a successful soldier. (Hear, hear). I do not think that I need enter into any details of the analysis as to what franchise should there be for women. But I will say this that man ought to share with woman all his rights. He should remember the immutable principle that woman has equal rights with man. Her right is slumbering—is almost in a moribund condition; but it has to be revived. Man must recognize that he and woman come to the door of death to create a nation. Like the right of man, hers is also the right to see how her nation shall live, how her nation shall sacrifice and how her nation shall uphold its honour.

Remember that it is for the honour of the nation that the Indian womanhood day after day comes to the gate of death, so that the Indian people may be born a million times free (loud cheers).

The Rowlatt Bills and Satyagraha

A public meeting of the citizens of Madras was held on 17 March 1919 at the beach opposite to the Presidency College, to urge on the Government to drop the Rowlatt Bills and to express its unqualified adherence to Mr. Gandhi's Satyagraha movement. Sarojini Naidu moved the following Resolutions:

(a) 'That this public meeting of the citizens of Madras once again earnestly urges on H. E. the Viceroy and the Government of India that they should drop the Rowlatt Bills, at least at this stage inasmuch as they are unjust, subversive of the principle of liberty and justice and destructive of the elementary rights of individuals on which the safety of the community as a whole and the state itself is based.

(b) That this public meeting gratefully welcomes the happy news of the arrival of Mahatma Gandhi tomorrow and once again expresses its unqualified adherence to Mahatma Gandhi's Satyagraha movement and calls on all the people to support it.

In moving these Resolutions, she said:

Citizens of Madras, you will wonder in what capacity and by what right I stand before you today to move the resolutions that the President of this evening has read out to you and also to interpret to you the meaning, the purpose, and the mission of what my honoured Guru, Mahatma Gandhi, has said to you (cheers). Ever since, in far-off Ahmedabad, in that little, thatched cottage where the selfless sage dwells, living the life of a self-chosen poverty, ever since the little Guru of the men and women came to decide that the only possible weapon today in the armoury for tyrannized India was not the weapon of the machine guns and swords but the immortal, elementary, and invincible weapon of all spiritual revolt against temporal iniquity and therefore we few men and women realizing that, always in the spirit, there has been a channel of spiritual revolt and spiritual power which is against the material weapon and the material power of other nations, we decided to dedicate our lives and all that our lives stand for in the way of our personal liberty and yea, according to the world's standards, of our personal honour and our personal happiness. Since then I found there have been misconceptions of all kinds that reached me from the far off quarters of India where my friends are scattered. They ask, 'Why have you not made an All India movement? Why have not the leaders in all parts of India been consulted? Why is there no organization, cut and dried, such as the All-India Congress Committee organization? Why has this not been carried on exactly on those mechanical lines of progression such as all constitutional and traditional political agitation is carried on?' And they say to me, 'Is it fair, is it right, that behind our backs, without our knowledge, you and your friends should have started this fire, this conflagration of the spirit of India? Is it right that while we politicians are using those acknowledged and accredited weapons of political agitation, while the traditional methods of appeal, of memorials, of protests, and of resolutions, are still being carried on throughout the length and breadth of India, that this Satyagraha should have been launched upon our wondering and discomfited world?' The answer is simple, but it is final since it is comprehensive; for the Satyagraha movement is a thing of organic life which must of necessity grow and expand because it carries within itself the immortal functions of life and so the Satyagraha Movement has kindled its fire in the temple or ashrams where Mahatma Gandhi is the high priest or Guru. He has lighted the flame where the torches of the spirits of India must catch fire so that in the spiritual illumination of that national dedication to the cause of justice and liberty, India shall be served by her great army of spiritual warriors ready for death. That, gentlemen, is the meaning of Satyagraha.

It has been said to me, and I am here as it were to accept the challenge and to answer it, and I shall answer it to your satisfaction, I am told that what you propose as the Satyagraha movement means the disruption of national life as constitutionally carried on. It means the disintegration of all political work, it means the placing of a dangerous instrument of power in the hands of all those who are unaccustomed to the discipline and the responsibility of power. I am told also that in disobeying laws, however unjust, we are creating a perilous and far-reaching tradition of evil, in teaching irreverence for constituted law and authority. We are told that in playing upon the spiritual instincts and emotions of an emotional people like the Indians, we are creating that which many generations might not effectually be able to ameliorate in the way of revolution. We are told that we are creating a precedent that will land in every kind of danger and disintegration, if not death, to us and to others of our tradition which will make what is called in English language (since it is so poor) passive resistance and in the tongues of our forefathers, Satyagraha. It will create a tradition of lawlessness, a tradition that will always use this resistance against every kind of authority that may not for the moment appeal to us. All these criticisms and these comments have but one answer. That logic, that law, is not the ultimate standard of a nation's spiritual advancement. There are times in the history of nations, as of individuals, when the customary law of caution, of order, of reverence to constituted authority must fail before the inspiration and the impulse and the intuition of the moment's demand. Sirs, if logic, if mere reasoning, if the mere academic following of things to their logical conclusions were always the highest mode of achievement, would the French nation have been led to victory if the soldiers of France had never been guided by the tactics and strategy (and not authority) and by the historic vision of that hysteric woman Joan of Arc, 'Follow me, the "vision of truth"?' It was the thought of that vision of the destiny of France, that vision of faith in the strategy of the French General that gave the victory to the French nation and created the heroine for the inspiration of the years to come. Take our own history. If always and at all times we had been guided by our traditional meekness, by our traditional acceptance of all that comes from above, whether of kings or of gods, had we today been alive as the Hindu nation, a nation keeping on against tremendous odds, by century after century of foreign domination, had we been today a living people, shall we give up Satyagraha, i.e., (passing resistance) which we have adopted age after age against a law subversive of the tradition and the civilization and the spirit of the Indian people? No! Therefore when they say to us that Satyagraha is a new weapon translated into modern Indian tongues, they say something that is not true, for the great law of Satyagraha is the very instinctive law of self-defence against aggression and against tyranny that we Indians have followed, because Satyagraha is that form of historic resistance to outside devastating and disintegrating influences which has kept the life and spirit of Indian people today. Laws were made and they were obeyed age after age and century after century, while those laws were justly made even by an alien Government for the protection and well-being of a subject people. But can you think, you descendants of Brahminical sires, you descendants of those who were conquered by the Islamic spirit, can you remember a single instance in your own history when the law being unjust and subversive of your spiritual traditions, of that honour which is higher to you than life, is there a single instance when you have not resisted as a people? Do not you remember that when in Rajputana where honour was considered greater than life, what did the women of Rajputana do when their honour was threatened? They went in their hundreds, like brides, in the funeral pyre, so that the honour of the Rajput race might be inviolate. And what women could do, a handful of Rajput women could do, for the honour which was the ideal of their race, surely must be to you the lesson or inspiration; for today you are threatened not merely in your material interests, you are threatened not merely in your temporal interests, but you are threatened with a legislation which implies and which must imply the climax of all degradation that you have been enduring in the past and which they have bestowed on you as the crowning insult of insults, the crowning tyranny of tyrannies, and which will make you unable to lift your head because, you, in accepting, in acquiescing in that unjust tyranny will have lost your primeval right to be called men, men of honour, to whom their self-respect is greater than the favour of kings. Therefore, friends, the Satyagraha has been started, but it does not for one single instance arrogate to itself a function that brings it into conflict with other and older and more familiar, and

more (so-called) constitutional—I will say traditional—
forms of protest and agitation, it does not arrogate to
itself a superiority from the merely expedient, merely
temporary political standpoint. For, what has been the
history of Indian politics? For generations, it has been
faced with a new set of problems, a new set of laws, it
has had to get accustomed to a new set of tyrannies from
a new set of laws, age after age. But there is something
in life that is greater than politics; for politics in its very
nature must be transient, must be determined and limited
by circumstances either local or world-wide. Politics are
temporary and transient problems of today which make
obsolete similar problems of yesterday and in their turn
give place to wider, more difficult and more complex
problems of tomorrow. But more than the politics of a
race are the ideals of a race, the rights, the privileges, the
duties, and responsibilities of a race. There are laws which
are man-made. Laws in their very nature, being man-
made like politics, changed from age to age according
to circumstances and environments. But there is law and
there is justice, sometimes, and my lawyer friends will
pardon a mere ignoramus for making such an assertion.
In the name of justice, its antonym, blind injustice, is
done which the heart of man cannot endure. For justice is
primordial, justice is deep-rooted in the very life of man,
not to be determined by one race or another, not to be
translated in the terms of one language or another, nor
to be measured by the superiority of one conquering race
over another.

Law is that which a governing race may make the voice of one people that is clear in itself, each implying a certain responsibility to the other, each carrying within itself a certain function of steadfast and faithful duty towards the other. But in India the whole history of our country have been a series of compromises between the conquering people and the conquered race whereby the conquered people have perforce acquiesced for the peace and artificial security of the state, because it took for granted the good faith of the conquering race and they would in return for the acquiescence in law, in themselves unjust, and of a merely expedient kind they have accepted from the other party to the treaty their good faith and good intention for the legislation of the land. Such laws I need not today enumerate to you. All of us have instances, in our mind of the laws in recent times in which we acquiesced with burning hearts and indignation, indeed acquiesced because they seemed necessary as temporary measures, or so at least our rulers told us. But when you come to a legislation which in its very nature is universally counted to be subversive against all laws of God and subversive of all human rights of man, whether he be of the Slav-nationality of which we had never heard before or small, poor, down-trodden nationality which we all share, we are called upon to follow, to give loyalty at least in this measure to Government which is disloyal to the pact made (cheers) to urge its own ideals, the very traditions which made the British nation great. Englishmen in their heart of hearts

are ashamed of all form of tyranny, for remember that
the great boast of the British people has been this, that
England is a land of liberty and in England the exiles
of liberty from other lands have found shelter and were
honoured. Mazzini, Garibaldi, Kossuth, Kuropatkin,
these are honoured exiles of liberty, the revolutionaries
of their own land, they were honoured by the kings of
that constitutional monarchy. The poets of England,
Swinburne, Landor, Shelley, Byron, Milton, to go back
in anti-climax of greatness, have all written in honour
of those who, deserving the exclusion of politics in their
own land, were given a seat of honour by the kings and
by statesmen in England. And how can it be said that
there is one law of honour for those who love liberty and
fly to England from Italy or Russia and only the present
laws of degradation for those who in India say, 'May I
India, for your liberty give my life and for your honour
let me drop this my frame'? This, friends, is exactly what
is happening today. In the Viceroy's Council, Sir William
Vincent and the other great men whose coffers have been
filled these many years from the wealth of India, boast
that England went to war in this great worldwide War
because of her chivalry towards a weak neutral nation,
that England would be paramount in this great League of
Nations that is to determine the exact place and purpose,
the exact balance of power, of freedom, of prestige
which go to belong to any of the nations of the world.
When it comes to India, it says, 'My dependency, our
Allies are the Belgians whom we have championed, the

Colonies beyond the seas we hold as comrades of our blood, America has our blood, our kin, our friends and our colleagues in this Great War of freedom. But you sent your sons to France, sent the blood of your blood to Flanders, the soul of your souls in the life-giving stream into the deadly deserts of Arabia and for your reward take this stigma, this brand of dishonour of the fallen, unable to rise because you are unarmed.' This is the brand of the man who cannot rise up and say, 'I have my place in the League of Nations', my voice must raise the echo of music in that great centre of harmony that you call the Peace Conference. But no. The vocabularies of freedom have been re-edited by liberal men, the vocabularies of liberty have been printed in a limited edition for circulation only among those who belong to one colour, creed of the world. And yet loyalty is in that dictionary that is printed for slaves like us. Contentment is another word. Loyalty, contentment, and gratitude are the assets of a conquered nation, while power, honour, freedom, prestige are rights of a nation that holds your heart under its heel. Not to us belong the weapons of Europe, the swords forged into the death of man. We children of a great spiritual tradition of sacrifice, have one weapon left only, not machine guns that mow down thousands from far, not bayonets that tear open the entrails of a small race, we have only the weapon of suffering, the weapon of sacrifice, the weapon of dauntless self-determination which means to most of us death in some form or other. That is the only weapon in the armoury of the world's weapons left to us. It is that weapon alone which will lead us to victory, for to each race is given its own form of triumph, its own form of battle, its own vision, its own liberty, its own privilege to conquer and die. To us is given the great privilege of dying. We say we watch the agony of our fellow men, we share the destiny of sacrifice of our brothers. It all means suffering and death to us. That is the weapon of Satyagraha to which Mahatma Gandhi bids you come. For he says we will follow the truth fearlessly. We all know that truth is most elusive and most beckoning and dauntlessly beckons layers of the human mind in the path of truth, in the path that we shall follow. It means that at every step we may be called upon to test the sincerity of our conviction, the glory of our invincible courage. It means that we shall be called upon to give up not merely the lands that our fathers have left us, the gold that we have gained by our labours, more than this it is possible, it is likely that we shall be called upon to lose some of those we love best, our children, our mothers, our wives, our brothers, and yet the individual suffering, the individual sacrifice must be less than it is in your eyes if your renunciation of all fame, of all gain, of all love, of all liberty, means for the generations to come a legacy of liberty which you shall have earned for your suffering and sacrifice (cheers). Let constitutional agitation follow the traditional channels. Let rhetoric upon rhetoric and memorials of protest flow to the wide sea that brings up the waves of Bills which answers nothing. Let there be this logical, reasonable statesmanship. Let there be the old,

gentle, courteous, reasonable, and ambassadorial powers
of negotiation given to our ambassadors of liberty. We
are not ambassadors. We are not for the moment at least
mere statesmen. We are soldiers of a great spiritual army.
The standard of that army is the wrath born of sacrifice.
We are told that this law is to be confined to criminals. So
far as it is urged in that very preposterous and monstrous
declaration, brings within the folds of its proclamation
the most innocent child of our household, it has dwindled
and dwindled for reasons of statesmanship probably for
reasons born of ambassadorial negotiations, may be of
expediency—I do not know not being in the secrets of the
Imperial Council and Councillors.

It says that the law will apply in its final stage to
criminals and to areas where anarchy is rife or has been
rife, where the soil though barren might still perhaps
yield the vital seeds of anarchy within the soil. But what
is anarchy except the gift of Europe to India, disrupted
by the European Government? Where was anarchy in
the traditions of India of sacrifice? But anarchy is the
expression of Western people driven and goaded to
desperation beyond the limits of human endurance and
if today here and there be anarchy in this land, is it not
that a government being anarchical to its own traditions
of liberty brought anarchy to the heart of liberty and
justice more than life (cheers)? Secret legislation must
result in secret revolution (laughter), Injustice must bring
disloyalty to the hand that destroys what is finer and
diviner than a man can conceive, Anarchy in Bengal and

in Maharashtra! Why not? If the legitimate hope of youth be driven under unto a living grave, if the legitimate and good instinct for progress and liberty, that honourable and necessary instinct of man for freedom within his own land be not accepted and honoured as a right as proper and honourable, but is chastised, persecuted and driven underground, what is the result? Miasma and Malaria are the results of stagnant waters that have no channels to flow. But running water is always sweet. The rivers of life become the sanctuaries of all men's hopes. If the Ganga had been still and the Jumna had been stagnant, how do these two divine rivers that flow through the spiritual civilization of our land stay to us as the symbols of progress in all divine achievements and attempts? Even so the life of man flows and should flow unhampered with the Ganga and Jumna sweet always, shining always, carrying on its broad breast hopes and fears, the prayers and desires of man. But our hopes, our fears, our struggles, our demands at unity and the divine things for which every land and every race has been honoured, have been put into a living grave and heaped up with stones and stones of tyranny but waters can flow underground. Here and there where there is no depth one gets stagnation but there are times, there are places in the world where there are secret waters flowing and flowing in the darkness and one day they burst the bond of secrecy and find somehow the predestined seas of their achievement. So today all our hopes are hidden underground, all our aspirations are driven underground that have been covered up and buried in graves that extend miles and miles. It is said that life has ceased within us and that our hopes are dead within us. Rather it means that all the impulses have been submerged and have at last come together to a point of unity and somehow will burst their bonds and flow into their predestined ocean of liberation. That is why we say that when all things fail in India, that silent faith which is born of the spirit of courageous sacrifice will not fail. If men say that they prefer the familiar and the safer paths of their traditional methods, we say, 'Brothers, good cheer to you. Follow the ways of your conviction. If there be those in our midst who say that we have the conviction of the truth, we have that courage of the truth but we are fettered hand and foot by fetters not forged by Government but by our loved ones whose love depends upon our freedom and ability to serve them.' To serve them, to them we say, 'You too are of our army and serve us in your own place. Do not share with us in the result of your conviction and courage but stand aside and do your duty in your place. Give to us the benediction of your support, the prayers that will sustain us in our labour. If we fail, do not condemn the failure but rather praise us when we have in our failure raised a great spiritual army of men and women that count life less than their honour so that the star of your freedom may rise.' It is not every man and every woman that is called to this great army of workers. It is not the destiny to suffer death. When I say death, I do not mean the death of the body which brings disintegration and putrefaction of flesh in three days'

time. I mean in that widespread and profound sense of
the disintegration of worldly life which might follow you
to the very end; for, remember that the standard of the
world and of the spirit are diverse things. Men according
to worldly ideas judge you by the houses you have built,
by the gold in your coffers, by the titles showered upon
you, but those who judge success by the endeavour of
man know that man is God and every effort of his to fulfil
that God-head within him is the true way of Satyagraha
of which Mahatma Gandhi speaks. If, as I say, in the
following of Satyagraha we choose deliberately to destroy
those laws which we think in their very nature are the
children of tyranny and oppression, is there any in your
midst so narrow and conventional as to pay reverence to
man-made authority or so cowardly in his consistency
who will dare to say to us, 'You are infringing our
moral laws'? There are laws that are coeval with the life
of man and coeval with the birth of man's conscience,
which belong to no age and to no race, but is equally
the inheritance of man to be safeguarded, enriched and
handed down from generation to generation, radiant
and insistent. Other laws are man-made, the offspring of
expediency, of temporary necessities, of emergencies, and
sometimes of that 'might' which we have not been able
to resist. If in the pursuit of a battle against a profound
and far-reaching threat of tyranny, not for one year or
two years or even the acknowledged three years of its
legislative powers which means death to every national
idea of self-respect and progress in your heart, if we break

these laws we are not criminals, we are not doing what is illegitimate, but we are exercising that self-determination of which the Peace Conference has said so much. If we are determined, then at all costs, we will win freedom for ourselves. We will not leave to the generation yet unborn a legacy of shame because we have failed to be strong and because we cannot endure that our children's children should rise up and say, 'Oh! traitors to your past. Oh! traitors to our future, for the sake of a little personal security and comfort did you pre-ordain shame to us, did you go back upon the great tradition that your forefathers left to you in trust for us.' Because we cannot endure the stigma of dishonour in the future, the stigma of shame today, that we followers of Sityagraha, the spiritual soldiers of truth ask you if you people come and fight side by side with us with that sword that is of the spirit, well and good, but if you cannot come with us in that great battle of pilgrimage, if you cannot share with us in that work, stand aside, not in mockery of us, not in opposition to us. Who are you that cannot accept our truth and yet make mockery of our conviction? Stand aside from the pilgrimage of the soldiers of truth. But if you share with us in the vision of that liberty which is your birthright, even though you cannot share with us the sufferings of our pilgrimage, cheer us in our way, give us your benediction, and bid us be of good cheer, because we fight for your and your children's children and that honour which is India's and shall be India's, if we and this generation die to achieve freedom (cheers).

The Punjab Tragedy

At the Kingsway Hall, London, on 3 June 1920, Sarojini Naidu made the following speech on the tragedy of Punjab. This speech was the subject of an animated debate in the Commons and a heated correspondence between Mr. Montagu and Sarojini Naidu:

My compatriots, I do not speak to you tonight, but for you Englishmen and Englishwomen, I speak to you today as standing arraigned at the bar because of the blood guiltiness of those who have committed murder in my country. I need not go into detail about these incredible atrocities that have been committed. My friends Mr. Patel and Mr. Horniman, have already given you in outline and in essence the nature of that horrible, most horrible, thrice horrible deed, done in the name of British justice. But I am going to speak to you as a woman, about the wrongs committed against my sisters. Englishmen, you who pride yourselves upon your chivalry, you who hold more precious than all your Imperial treasures the honour and the chastity of your women, will you sit still and leave unavenged the dishonour, and the insult, and the agony inflicted upon the veiled women of the Punjab?

One of the speakers has said that Lord Chelmsford
refused to draw the veil from the ugly face of realities;
but his minions, his martial authorities rent the veil from
the faces of the women of the Punjab. Not only were
the men mown down as if they were grass that is born
to wither, but they tore asunder the cherished purdah,
that innermost privacy of the chaste womanhood of
India. If you look into the pages of the Report drawn up
by my own compatriots you will find in it that women
who had never been seen or heard by a stranger, women
whose faces had never been touched even by the curious
sun or the moon, were dragged into the market place.
Englishmen and Englishwomen, my sisters were stripped
naked; they were flogged; they were outraged; and yet
you dare to talk of the auction of souls. The auction of
souls was the auction of your British souls, your British
democracy betrayed and dishonoured, for no dishonour
clings to the martyrs who suffered, but to the tyrants who
inflicted the tyranny and pain.

I ask you one question only. Would you hold your
Empire by a dishonour on the womanhood of another
race or would you rather lose your Empire out of chivalry
for the honour and chastity of another nation? That is the
question that was asked many centuries ago in your own
Scriptures: 'What shall it profit a man to gain the whole
world and lose his own soul?' You deserve no Empire.
You today have lost your soul; you today have the stain of
blood-guiltiness upon you; you today are in the position
of the arraigned. What is your plea for reprieve? What is

your plea for pardon? What is your place today among the honourable nations of a free world? No nation that rules by tyranny is free; it is the slave of its own despotism.

One of the minions of Martial Law said to defenceless women, from whom all their men folk up to seven and eight years old had been taken: 'Swine, if I shoot you what will you do?' I say in reply: 'Swine, if you shoot us, we shall live! You can kill our bodies but our souls go free!' Cry shame upon tyranny! Peace for the martyrs in some generation to come! An opportunity to wash out your blood-guiltiness by the tears of your own women martyred like ours!

Speech at the Ahmedabad Congress

In supporting Mahatma Gandhi's call for the country to prepare for civil disobedience, Sarojini Naidu spoke as follows at the Ahmedabad Congress in December 1921:

Citizens of the India of which we dream today, but which we shall achieve tomorrow, you have heard representatives of all the great religions of India today. You have heard the Moslem, the Hindu and the Sikh. You have heard the men and the women speak. I speak not as representing any religion, any province, any sex today, but arrogant as it might seem, in all humility, I say, I speak as the Spirit of Free India. (Hear, hear)

Therefore, I stand up to offer my support to this great resolution which has been placed before you not in the manner of resolutions of 36 years' experience of resolutions from the platform of the National Congress, but which has been thundered out to you with the voice of a prophet from the mountain top of vision and of hope (cheers). I am not one who cares for Governments or authorities. I care only for principles and ideals. I am not one who panders to expediencies. I acknowledge and follow only the wisdom of the ever-living Truth.

Therefore, if I stand before you to speak, it is because I am the voice of your own heart, the very innermost secret surging voice of your own conscience, your own aspirations, your own hopes, your own certainty.

What does this resolution say? What does it mean? What challenge does it throw? What does it affirm? What does it deny? It denies the right of the most powerful Government on earth to trample on the heart and soul of a living nation. What does it affirm? It affirms, in the words of Lokmanya Bal Gangadhar Tilak, that 'liberty is our birthright,' and we shall have liberty today? What is the challenge thrown to the Government? It says, as Mahatma Gandhi so wonderfully put it, that the door is open. March with us to that destined goal that we see before us today when you and your children, Rulers of Britain, might eclipse side by side with us in friendship and comradeship! But unless you realise that it is not by the might of the sword but by the invincible, slender, fragile, silken cord of love that nations can be bound together, you have no place in our midst.

And what is the answer to repression? The answer is that those dozens of delicately nurtured women who, having sent their sons, husbands, and fathers to prison, have come today to take their place to carry on the torch in the words of Deshbandhu Chitta Ranjan Das, to be the pilgrims on the road and to build up the edifice of your freedom with their corpse if death be necessary. As soon might you tell the sun not to rise at dawn as to say to India, 'Don't move towards your destined freedom.'

As soon might you say to the Ganges, 'Cease to flow' as to say to the sacred spirit of Indian womanhood, 'Don't flow towards the sea of Liberty.' You might as well say to the earth, 'Cease to flower in the spring', and to the stars in the sky at midnight, 'Don't shine,' as to say to the young ones amongst us, 'Don't join the volunteer corps.' Do I not know what the younger generation can endure, what it can achieve? During those dreadful few days in Bombay when it seemed that the whole of our work was to be cast in ruins, who was it that saved the situation? Who, not only the fast of the saint within his cell but the endurance, the courage, the sacrifice of my young volunteers—who stood, night and day fearlessly, bloodshed around them, death around them, disaster around them, but true to their post, the symbol of the Indian victory? Therefore I do not share the fear of Shree Shankaracharya nor of anyone else who thinks that India will give her divided support to this proposition. There is no division in India today, no caste, no tradition of caste. No tyranny of caste can keep the untouchables from being the comrade, and the equals of the twice-born Brahmin in their march to freedom (hear, hear). Therefore, in the name of the young men of India, the young women of India, the old men and the old women of India, the oldest men and the oldest women of India, I pledge the lives, the Souls and all of every Indian to this great cause and say, 'In this great land, may there be peace because we win only through peace (continued applause).'

The Trial of Mahatma Gandhi

Sarojini Naidu was present at the Court when Mahatma Gandhi was tried and sentenced to six years' imprisonment. Describing the scene of the great trials in the Bombay Chronicle, *Mrs. Naidu wrote in March 1922:*

A convict and a criminal in the eyes of the Law! Nevertheless the entire Court rose in an act of spontaneous homage when Mahatma Gandhi entered—a frail, serene, indomitable figure in a coarse and scanty loin cloth, accompanied by his devoted disciple and fellow-prisoner, Shankerlal Banker.

'So you are seated near me to give me your support in case I break down,' he jested, with that happy laugh of his which seems to hold all the undimmed radiance of the world's childhood in its depths. And looking round at the hosts of familiar faces of men and women who had travelled far to offer him a token of their love, he added, 'This is like a family gathering and not a law-court.'

A thrill of mingled fear, pride, hope and anguish ran through the crowded hall when the Judge took his seat— an admirable Judge deserving of our praise alike for his brave and resolute sense of duty, his flawless courtesy, his just perception of a unique occasion and his fine tribute to a unique personality.

The strange trial proceeded and as I listened to the immortal words that flowed with prophetic fervour from the lips of my beloved master, my thoughts sped across the centuries to a different land and different age when a similar drama was enacted and another divine and gentle teacher was crucified, for spreading a kindred gospel with a kindred courage. I realised now that the lowly Jesus of Nazareth cradled in a manner furnished the only true parallel in history to this sweet invincible apostle of Indian liberty who loved humanity with surpassing compassion and to use his own beautiful phrase, 'approached the poor with the mind of the poor.'

The most epic event of modern times ended quickly.

The pent-up emotion of the people burst in a storm of sorrow as a long, slow procession moved towards him in a mournful pilgrimage of farewell, clinging to the hands that had toiled so incessantly, bowing over the feet that had journeyed so continuously in the service of his country.

In the midst of all this poignant scene of many voiced and myriad hearted grief he stood, untroubled, in all his transcendent simplicity, the embodied symbol of the Indian Nation—its living sacrifice and sacrament in one.

They might take him to the utmost ends of the earth but his destination remains unchanged in the hearts of his people who are both the heirs and the stewards of his matchless dreams and his matchless deeds.

Trivandrum Speech

As the Trivandrum Aryachalai Hall, where Sarojini Naidu delivered the following speech on Sunday, 18 October 1922, had become dark owing to heavy rains and as the immense crowd who thronged around the hall for want of space inside had obstructed the light from every aperture of the hall, the audience cried for light. As soon as Sarojini Naidu ascended the platform she said:

Friends, your cry for light, light, light, reminds me of the great German poet who said 'more light, more light.' It reminds me of the holy message that I have come to deliver to you summed up in one great word, 'more light' for the people of my country (hear, hear and cheers). I have come as one in your midst not to seek honour at your hands. Not for a single moment did I suppose that, coming quietly, and, as I thought, to arrange and restore light, did I expect that I should have the opportunity and privilege to deliver to the people of this city the great immortal message that it is my special charge to carry from city to city, from village to village, from deserts to mountain-tops and from the snow-clad peaks of the Himalayas to the lowest plains (cheers). The message such as I have to give you, not my own, but as the mouth piece of that great man, my master (hear, hear) whose heart languishes in the high prison walls, whose deed, whose word, whose glory, whose compassion, whose sacrifice, whose love had gone up, unrepressed and irrepressible by the might of the English nation—whether of God or of man or devil upon this earth (hear, hear). I have lately come here on a double pilgrimage, from Ceylon, where, as we read, the message of Buddha, still lives among the promiscuous remains of that royal city. I have come also after fulfilling my religious duty at Rameswaram where Rama celebrated his victory of the deliverance of the ideal of Indian womanhood, Sita, from the clutches of Ravana; and today with the benediction of the double pilgrimage to the temple where Rama made his offering to the great God and the lost City of Anuradhapura where every full moon night chastens the bodies of men and women, who pay their offerings to the temple of Him who was the precursor of my master, I must feel a special responsibility in speaking to you and ask God to touch my lips with fire so that I might deliver a right to you, what he, that is reincarnate Buddha, says to a suffering people. When I see this surging wave of enthusiasm, when I see your devotion for the word of Mahatma Gandhi, breaking around me in peals of passionate admiration and applause, I say to myself—need I go to the temple of Kanyakumari? I see the waves of the amazing ocean break around me here and surge amid waves of many hearts and many souls ready to acknowledge that great word that has gone forth, of love, and sacrifice, of austerity, of suffering, of redemption through penance, for deliverance through that great power of which words form the embodied symbol. Smaller than myself, so frail that his body trembles like the leaf in the Bo-tree, so solemn, so indomitable that even the greatest among men fail to reach, even as the brave explorers have failed to reach the topmost peak of Mount Everest!

Friends, what is this message that Mahatma Gandhi has brought to a suffering, waiting world? No more than the paraphrase, no more than the practical realisation of the great motto which presides over your own city, that 'Charity is our household divinity.' (Applause) For, what is charity? St. Paul, around whose historic name is seen the rich controversy in your city, said that there were three great things, Faith, Hope and Charity, of which 'Charity' is the greatest.

I have come to tell you of the fulfilment of that charity, that passion, that love which is uppermost, the fulfilling of the law of life and therefore very near your own household divinity. Mahatma Gandhi, after his victorious martyrdom in South Africa, came back to his country, hoping that here, he who had been able in that far-off country, to make heroes out of common clay, in a land of the living he had men to work side by side, and shoulder to shoulder. But alas! When he returned with those feet weary of the pilgrimage of suffering, he found in a land that once had made heroes out of common clay, nothing but common clay waiting for him to remodel into heroes. He wandered throughout the length and breadth of this land, he studied and measured our academic work, our academic politics, our rhetoric, our proclamations, our resolutions, our protestations, and measured them by the only authentic standard, and that was the standard of those who starved and died in the famine-stricken villages of India; and measured by that pining and measured by hunger and agony, he knew how futile it is—how we do not want the generation of the world who dwelt in prosperous cities and in the leisure of prosperous lives, talked eloquently, but talked foolishly, but divorced from reality, of imaginary conditions, not having once crossed the threshold of agony, and he said that this is not what India is wanting, not this rhetoric of half-time, quarter-time, that which the holiday politician demands, but it demands whole-time education of men and women to a solution of the problem of poverty; because without the solution of that economic degradation and slavery of India, it is hopeless to talk of freedom at all, and because, he, living to the very heart of the hungry people of the country, to the very throbbing of the shivering body of the naked, realized that only true economic regeneration will give political liberty to India. He sent forth the mandate—Let there be Khadi throughout India—not the Khadi as coarse as this table cloth nor handspun Khadi exactly like this (gesturing to the cloth she was wearing), but only the symbol of that Swadeshi spirit which is the only symbol that a free Indian nation can possess. What is this Swadeshi spirit? What is it? Not merely the spinning-wheel in every house, not merely the donning of the livery of those who call themselves the followers of Mahatma Gandhi, not merely the arrogance of those who by their being clothed in homespun cloth think that they are greater than those who have not donned that cloth—for the simplicity that dwells in palaces is greater than the arrogance that walks in the highways.

Friends, Mahatma Gandhi's message has penetrated into every corner, not only of India, not only of Ceylon, not only of Europe, but to the remotest recess of every portion of the world's continent, where one single hungry, one single naked woman, one single starved child is alive to hear the message of deliverance. You living in the native states do not have the same need, the same justification for emphasising the political aspects of the movement. For well or for ill, for good or for evil, you and I subjects of Native States, have Swaraj; and it is not against our own governments that we are fighting, but it is against the spirit of alien administration which has no right in any land. You and I, therefore, as subjects of great Native States, have to devote our energies, our attention, our talents, our experiments, our achievements to these four social aspects of the great Satyagraha Movement, always realising that the social aspects are the essential aspects of any movement in this world. What are the fourfold aspects with which this movement deals?

The Swadeshi spirit covers literally all the many manifestations of the movement, and yet, though the word Swadeshi covers three-fourths of the entire spirit of

India, I will nonetheless divide it by analysing it into four paramount portions that you must in this Province, this kingdom of Travancore, try to realise it with all practical effect. Swadeshi in India, I mean in those parts of India which are no Native States, deals primarily with the hand at the spinning-wheel in the homes of those brothers who are troubled by poverty and disease. The spinning for the woman in the house of the peasants is really more than the jewels that your sisters and many others of the richer classes may invest against rainy days; for the spinning is a sign and symbol that the crushing poverty of the people is no more, and the money-lender does not suck the life-blood of the poor agriculturist. I know and you know too, if you read history aright, that from immemorial times, the spinning-wheel has been the supplementary source of income for all the Indian villages, and I might say for the whole of India, because we of the towns count for less than nothing when the overwhelming portion of the people of India are among those that dwell in the moffusil. Sow the wind and reap the whirlwind sometimes, but nonetheless suffer physical, mental and moral degradation. We have sown and reaped our industries, our arts, and all the pride of our own past generation, so inextricably bound up with the great art of spinning which you know was crushed because of the need of those East India Company people, to promote the economic interests of Lancashire. You know that terrible story of the fine silk of Murshidabad, the beautiful mull and the Dacca muslin, whose fine texture and variety of colour and design were exterminated. The looms and even the fingers of the manufacturers were cut off, and crushed and in their crushing was involved the prosperity of the agricultural classes. You know too the degradation that has come by their wearing the livery of a subject nation. Princess Mary of England was a truer Swadeshi than any of you who say 'Mahatmaji-ki-Jai.' Her wedding garments were not made out of foreign looms but made by the hands of the poor peasant women in Ireland and Scotland, Wales and England. She wore the Khadi made in England as Mahatmaji wants everyone and every beggar to wear the Khadi of India. This movement of the spinning wheel is a movement for our regeneration because it brings to the women of the family, the protection to all those starving children who now endure scarcity of diet, the only remains of the matter that appear, besides the growing for the sustenance by these mothers who are not more than living skeletons. Therefore the very centre of the Swadeshi movement is the spinning-wheel. In spinning, you will ask me, 'Why not mills?' Surely they provide livelihood for a few thousands of men living in horrid, unhealthy insanitary places, and the profits go to the pockets of the mill-owners; but the hand spinning—I am sure, women in your own home, good wives, true mothers are earning thereby, all the price for all their clothes. She need not go into the marketplace of great cities to pawn honour and chastity, to buy bread for her starving children. This is the meaning of the spinning-wheel. Mahatmaji says that it is the custodian of woman's honour. This is what he means when he compares a woman (who, having nothing to purchase her wherewithal owing to our indifference and criminal neglect) to Sita to save whose honour Rama struggled against Ravana when he was called forth to prove and vindicate the honour of a woman.

My friends, but the Swadeshi movement does not end merely with the wearing of Khadi and the spinning of Khadi to a large extent for a single item of our life. Let us remember that the Khadi we are wearing is no more than the simple repatriation of the traditions and ideals of our own country. Let us make it a centre round which the great artistic revival of India can be born. Let us make it the focus towards which the national forces may be drained and consecrated. Our literature, our music, our philosophy, our art, all the great contributions we have got to make to the world, let them be focussed, let them be symbolised, made holy by this symbol. The coarse cloth we have originally made becomes the very insignia of loyalty, because the kings themselves can do no better than to be patriots, as my own King in Hyderabad has done (cheers). Swadeshi does not end with that I told you; the cloth weaving and spinning is only one aspect of the Swadeshi movement. The other aspect of the matter, the diviner aspect of the movement as it seems to Mahatma Gandhi is the weaving and spinning of that rakhsha bandhan out of love and passion that binds to us in indissoluble brotherhood, those who are today the outcastes of Hindu society (hear, hear). While your women spin the thread and your weavers weave the doth in the looms, if in your own hearts you spin the thread of destiny and weave the fabric of liberty, then the Indian nation might be clothed with the name of the unified people. This question of untouchability is a very sore one, I am very much unpopular by always defending the down-trodden as against those of my own caste, who are the tyrants of the world, but I do not care for popularity. I care rather for the truth and I will proclaim it in any assembly of kings. I will speak for those who are born with the same travails of their mothers' wombs, brought up in the same sacrifice of their mothers, enduring the same human emotions, feelings and temptations, capable of the same heroism, knowing the same divine forgiveness. To suit your kind, you have hay, you have straw, you have fodder at least for fulfilling the letter of law in your religion. You set apart at your meal time a portion for the crow and portion for the dog, but you are so careful that you do not give to your own brother even the right that belongs with crow and the dog to share with you. My friends, until and unless this problem of the untouchables is solved, now and now and now, there is no tomorrow for this doomed race, unless it is tempted by the ideals of the younger races, struggling for the brotherhood of the world (hear, hear).

The third great portion of Mahatmaji's message deals with the question of temperance. I am not going to deal with the question of temperance today; for it will be an insult to my audience, but I want you to understand that the poor man at whom you point your finger of scorn, to shelter himself from the reach of hunger, gets drunk and we find him rolling in the gutter. I remember what these poor people have said to me. They said that it was cheaper to get drunk for a few pies and to forget the hunger than to remember it like you who have no temptation to forget it. Please remember that the remedy for intemperance is not in picketing but it is providing sufficient food for those rolling in gutters, forgetting their hunger, drunk, drunk, drunk. That is what I have to say about temperance.

Now there is one more point. That is National Education. Those of us who separate ourselves from the patriots who believe that National Education is the narrow patriotism that excludes great love for the cultures of the world, remember that that National Education and its ideals better form the traditions of the Hindu genius that assimilated from other sources, from friend and foe alike, transmitting, transfiguring by descent that foreign knowledge into national culture. Therefore we do not say we will not have the modern sciences of the West, the modern philosophy of the West, all the things that the younger world has to give for the land of the older world. It is an intellectual heritage which the unborn generations are entitled to for the intellectual progress of the world and for our National Education to be the finest expression of our national genius. By what are the divine laws, capacities and heroisms of our national genius, by what are the moral and the legal parts tenable, measurable by minimum standards? Let us remember that the present generation through these cultures of the West is only receiving back now what in the past, the earlier ages we gave in tenfold measure to the ancestors of this generation. Friends, I am a specialist in this matter of National Education. But to be merely national is to dig your own grave; but to be national, a united people might make great united contributions to the national wealth of the world. That is the justification of the nationalist today. It is only one stage in the great journey of India to the age of indivisible humanity and brotherhood of the world.

I have no more time, because I, who have been trying to tell you how Mahatmaji, my master, bids me proclaim your motto 'Charity, your household divinity,' I have great desire to pay my respects to your prince, your father who has proclaimed this great motto of charity as his household divinity. I am going to give him a paraphrase, an interpretation of the message which it has been my special privilege to deliver to the people of this company. I will make this one appeal to him who is the father of his people, who indeed metes out prosperity to his people in every department—allows them full and actual liberty, not merely the liberty to claim liberty, in every department as led by himself. When we began, we had to sit in darkness, but now light is come into this little room and I want all of you who have heard from me, in my poor faltering words, the message of my master to carry with you the kindling torch into the world, to relieve the poor downtrodden people who dare not come near you.

Even as many centuries ago, under the Bo-tree, came the revelation to Him they call Buddha, for the deliverance of human suffering, so has come the revelation to the person of my great master who says, 'Here my body is in prison, let the souls of all my people be free' (cheers).

Speech at Belgaum Congress

In moving the resolution on Indians overseas at the Belgaum Congress on 27 December 1924, Sarojini Naidu made out a strong case for the better treatment of Indians abroad. In the course of her speech, she said:

Friends, I have had to borrow Mahatmaji's glasses to read the resolution. I wish I have stolen a little of his wisdom and moderation as well. I will say a few words differing slightly from the resolution and mainly supporting it. I have recently returned from Africa to which you deputed me to go on your behalf and that, fresh in the memory of their disabilities and disadvantages, their sufferings and tyrannies from which our brethren and kindred are suffering. I feel, and Mahatma Gandhi will excuse me for feeling so, that this resolution is too little coloured with the life blood and with the suffering to which my people abroad are doomed. I feel so strongly on this matter that I would rather have been excused from speaking today where speeches must be so brief and so of that quality that might not divert too poignantly your minds from the central activity to which Mahatma Gandhi has made us pledge ourselves for the coming year. I think I should be failing in my duty were I not to supplement my own remarks to this resolution which I have the honour of moving and while I agree that till Swaraj is obtained in India we in the Congress cannot effectively help or come to the relief of the Indians overseas, I nevertheless believe that the Congress is a sufficiently powerful body to put such moral pressure upon the Imperial and Indian Governments that they should be compelled to do their duty by the people across the seas.

When I went to South Africa, when I was in the threshold of South Africa, while I was still in Portuguese East Africa, the South African people had sent their representative to interview me. One man, a little man, frank in his opinion, said to me, 'What will you do in South Africa, General Smuts is a strong man.' I said in reply, 'I am a strong woman with the whole weight of Indian opinion.' (Cheers.) It is the weight of Indian opinion behind me that took the message of hope to the suffering hearts from Mombasa to Cape Town. It was the same message I carried. The wonderful ovation I received was not for myself—nay, I was the embodied message of the nation of India (cheers).

Shall tyranny be over the people who are the blood, bone and the flesh of the people in India? It is carrying this message of hope, of kinship, of moral support, suffering with their suffering, rejoicing with their victories, that brought comfort, encouragement to the heart of Indians in Kenya and South Africa. While I condemn the Natal Government for passing an Ordinance so unconstitutional, doubly unconstitutional because I believe the taking away of the political franchise in 1896 from Indians was the first time almost in British history when a right that was given voluntarily was arbitrarily taken away and now this taking away of the municipal franchise is a betrayal of the Agreement arrived at with Mahatma Gandhi, it is more than that; it is a betrayal of the human inalienable rights of the Indian colonials who have as much right upon the African soil as General Smuts and other white colonials of South Africa. I believe it our duty to so create public opinion in the country that the Imperial and Indian Governments will be constrained not to be academic in their pity and compassion, but to protect effectively the interests of our brethren abroad.

Ever since I returned I have been pressing for a Round Table Conference, and when in South Africa I had the privilege of visiting the Ministers and Members of Parliament, I put forth the suggestion of a Round Table Conference. General Smuts and his party, General Hertzog and his party, Colonel Krassmann and his party were willing and anxious to consider this Round Table Conference, but the people of India failed because they did not sufficiently prove themselves in earnest in backing up the opinion of their own ambassador to South Africa. We in India have a power that we do not realise. One hundred and sixty thousand more or less exiled children of India are also being basely disinherited from the land where they have inviolable rights. Are we merely going to pass an academic resolution expressing helpless

lip sympathy? The white people deprive them of their
natural lights. This Natal Ordinance deprives them of
their inalienable rights. Are we to treat it as an academic
question saying it is merely a question of race prejudice
or are we going to solve it by going down to its roots and
help our brethren? I know my countrymen will be angry
with me for saying so. It is partly the economic pressure
in Natal that gives acuteness to the race feeling. Merely
saying it is race feeling will not help our brethren. They
look to us for more practical help to stretch out the hand
of fellowship which will enable them to stabilise their
moral position, to concentrate their moral strength and to
preserve the integrity of their ideal which bids them keep
alive and untainted the ideal of Indian heritage which is
theirs though they be colonial, coloured or white.

The Kenya question is a more recent question, a more
difficult question. Wherever it is economic pressure, it is
nothing but the Greed of the white settlers who want to
grab the whole of that fertile and fruitful country and
to create a black army against the peoples of Asia. I
feel there too we have neglected our duty, there too we
have been content with agitation on platforms. We were
outraged in our feelings because forsooth the highlands
were not given to the Indians. We were outraged in
our feelings because they proposed segregation. We
were outraged in our feelings, but after speeches were
made and resolutions recorded not one of us has had
the earnestness and honesty to pursue further with
indignation and put it into practical effect. Kenya, South

Africa and Mauritius or the Fiji and the Malaya States, the question remains the same, that colour prejudice is always there, that economic problem is always there, the disintegration of the people without a leader in the Colonies is always there. Since Mahatma Gandhi left Africa he left fatherless children and leaderless people. For the last 10 years these children have been groping and struggling in the dark. What have we done? So little have we concerned ourselves with the responsibility of our kinship. Almost like silent spectators we were not taking the trouble to shoulder some of their burdens and to give them that practical help which can go from India alone. No more than that we are helpless without Swaraj and we are helpless to a large extent without Swaraj. Can we not say 'no more emigration of labour, we shall feed our own people'? Now that Mahatma has given us the Mantra whereby no famine shall be in their land, shall we not say that we must not send cooks and clerks bound by an agreement to South Africa every year? We shall send educated men and women that still uplift the status of those people who are called cooks from Gandhi down to farm labourers who have built up Natal and who have built up the wealth of the white man. I said to General Smuts and General Hertzog, 'When you take your people back, then speak to me of taking my people back, not till then. Not even then shall my people be moved by force or fraud from this land where the bones of their fathers are testimony to the wealth of the white man. They have contributed to the wealth of the country by the sweat of their brow, to the progress of your plantations and they have heaped gold upon gold for you, victory upon victory, power upon power to tyrannise over the hand that feeds you.'

Are you in this Congress going out as messengers and ambassadors for helping the people overseas? Are you or are you not going to stop emigration of labour abroad? Are you so unpatriotic that your brethren must go abroad in shame and in sorrow and eat the bread of slavery because you will not solve the economic problems of India? I ask you, in supporting this resolution, in expressing your indignation, in condemning all these things to put forth your energy in removing the handicap upon our brethren abroad which deprives them of citizenship, of equal chances and of equal contribution to the civilisation of the Colonies. I ask you also to make it possible so that having won Swaraj by the strength of our united action we shall dare to lay down a law to the Government of the Colonies and say, 'At your own peril shall you touch the hair of my brother and only at your own risk you dare to challenge the manhood of the Indian nation.'

The Battle of Freedom Is Over

Sarojini Naidu delivered this speech on All India Radio on 15 August 1947, on the occasion of India's Independence:

Oh, world of free nations, on this day of our freedom, we greet you. Oh, world of nations not yet free, on the day of our freedom we pray for your freedom in the future. Ours has been an epic struggle, covering many years and costing many lives. It has been a struggle, a dramatic struggle. It has been a struggle of heroes chiefly anonymous in their millions. It has been a struggle of women transformed into strength and power like the Kali, the goddess of strength they worship. It has been a struggle of youth suddenly transfigured into power itself, sacrifice and ideals. It has been a struggle of young men and old men, of rich and poor, the literate, the illiterate, the stricken, the outcast, the leper and the saint. It has been the only revolution in the whole history of the world that has been without bloodshed; and for this we thank one man, one tiny person, who on this day that he has brought to us, is somewhat remote in a little far corner of India, wiping the tears of those who feel themselves exiled from our midst. Mahatma Gandhi, our prophet of non-violence, our general of victory, he taught us a new way of deliverance from evil. He had no device, of his banner excepting non-violence. He had no weapons for his legions excepting self-sacrifice and suffering. We marched to the tune of faith and hope; and charity that forgives all sins of trespassers that ruined our country through the ages. We have to thank him, our leader, whose life is immutable, immortal, in the love of his countrymen, whose days are imperishable, who has created a new civilization for the world to be based, in the years to come on his gospel of love, truth and non-violence.

But we wish to offer today our thanks to the men and women of all races who have striven for India's freedom, the scholars of Europe who restored to us our pride and ancient culture, to the antiquarian and the archaeologist who has discovered for us our own ruined cities, to the missionaries of all countries who chose the life of poverty in far-off villages and served the poor and the needy and the desolate. To all we owe thanks.

Today I remember those abroad who were the pioneers of our dream of freedom, men who are exiles if they are alive, forgotten if they are dead, who never sought nor received recognition nor reward, only privation, persecution and death. But all these today are immortal in our minds. We thank the Englishmen who were our friends, though many Englishmen were our enemies, not personal enemies but the victims themselves of a system of iniquitous imperialism. But those Englishmen who served us, become part of our Indian history, part of our struggle for India's Independence. And it seems somehow poetical, it seems somehow romantic, it seems somehow logical that the great-grandson of Queen Victoria, Louis Mountbatten, should have by grace and generosity, dissolved the empire that Disraeli built for her. All of them we thank.

The battle of freedom is over. The struggle for peace begins. And my country, my India, that has never excluded friend or foe from her hospitality, my India that has taken knowledge from all over the world once more will she stand in the forefront of world civilization, once more will she bring the message of peace, once more will she carry her lamp into the darkness of strife and struggle and hatred. And the nations of the world who are free, nations of the world who aren't free, we pledge you our comradeship, our fellowship, our understanding, our love. Let us work together towards the great world fellowship of which we dream. Let us work together for the peace that will never be ended. Let us work for justice, for equity, for human rights but no privileges, for human duties but no prerogatives, let us follow the citizens of a great free world of which our ancestors dreamed and for which we've striven. Men and women together, men and women of a common humanity, let no religion, no community, no text, no tongues divide us, for ours is a common destiny. Ours is a common purpose. Ours is a common wish and ambition to rebuild this broken world into the image of our heart's desire. And which

country but India can take the lead in restoring the world
to its pristine glory? We who have been the dreamers of
dreams, the seers of visions, the creators of wisdom, the
followers of renunciation, we, who have given the heroes
of independence struggle for India, we have run through
the whole gamut of the world's adventures, of the world's
emotions. We are the wise. We are reborn today of the
crucible of our sufferings.

Nations of the world, I greet you in the name of India,
my mother, my mother whose home has a roof of snow,
whose walls are of living seas, whose doors are always
open to you. Do you seek peace or wisdom, do you seek
love and understanding, come to us. Come to us in faith,
come to us in hope, come to us believing that all gifts are
ours to give. Today, in the name of India, I give for the
whole world the freedom of this India that had never died
in the past, that shall be indestructible in the future and
shall lead the world to ultimate peace.

LETTERS

Introduction to Letters

For over 50 years, Sarojini Naidu kept up a steady correspondence with all the people she was closely associated with. The letters picked for this collection provide a snapshot. The people these are addressed to were those who had an invaluable impact on her life and ideals. In some cases, their responses have also been included. The letters allow us to see a more personal side of her, and the writing differs quite significantly from her speeches and of course her poetry. We get a glimpse into the recollections of her daily life and the emotions she personally was dealing with. All of these allow us to form an idea of the kind of relationships she had with her friends, family and compatriot.

1.   Gandhiji to Sarojini Naidu, 18 November 1918

Dear Sister,

I appreciated your little note. I observe that you have survived the operation. I hope that it will be entirely successful, so that India may for many a year to come continue to hear your songs. For me I do not know when I shall be able to leave this sick-bed of mine. Somehow or other, I cannot put on flesh and gain more strength than I have. I am making a mighty attack. The doctors of course despair in face of the self-imposed restrictions under which I am labouring. I assure you that they have been my greatest consolation during this protracted illness. I have no desire whatsoever to live upon condition of breaking those disciplinary and invigorating restrictions. For me, although they restrict the body somewhat, they free the soul and they give me a consciousness of it which I should not otherwise possess. 'You can't serve God and Mammon' has a clearer and deeper meaning for me after those vows. I do not infer that they are necessary for all, but they are for me. If I broke them I feel that I should be perfectly worthless.

Do let me have an occasional line from you.

M.K. Gandhi

2. **Sarojini Naidu to Gandhiji, 17 July 1919**
   Duke's Hotel
   35 St. James's Place,
   London, S.W.1
   17th July, 1919

Dear Mr. Gandhi,

There is not much to report except that the evidence before the Joint Committee has begun and all our deputation will be called to give their evidence after the official witnesses have finished. I also expect to give evidence for the Women's Home Rule League separately and meanwhile I am forming a strong all-India non-party deputation to wait on the Secretary of State on the question of women franchise. Several attempts have been made to find common ground for all the deputations, but in vain so far. I think however they will all unite on the question of Rowlatt Act and the Punjab and send up a joint memorandum.

My health is very bad. The doctor thinks my heart is permanently damaged and can't get better (The X-ray shows a horrifying condition!!) but it can get worse! But my crippled condition is improving under treatment.

I see a woeful and even wilful ignorance and indifference about India in England—it is so precious to us, so rotten and valueless thing to them, except as enriching their coffers. But! The spirit conquers in the end!

I hope you are well. I have had no news from India at all. The post goes out at once.

So bandemataram!
Sarojini Naidu

3. **Sarojini Naidu to Gandhiji**
   Duke's Hotel,
   St James's Place,
   London SW1, 1920

My dear friend:

I have not written to you for a long time but you have been as usual in my thought and speech. I am in very bad health but the twin questions of the Punjab and the Khilafat absorb all my energies and emotions: but it is in vain to expect justice from a race so blind and drunk with the arrogance of power, the bitter prejudice of race and creed and colour, and betraying such an abysmal ignorance of Indian conditions, opinions, sentiments, and aspirations . . . The debate on the Punjab in the House of Commons last week shattered the last remnants of my hope and faith in British justice and goodwill towards the new vision of India . . . The discussion in the house was lamentable and indeed tragic: our friends revealed their ignorance, our enemies their insolence and the combination is appalling and heartbreaking.

Mr Montague has proved a broken reed . . . I enclose a copy of my correspondence with him on the subject of the outrages committed during (the) Martial Law regime upon women as embodied in the Congress Sub-committee's report and evidence. I naturally assume that no single statement contained in the evidence has been accepted without the most rigorous and persistent scrutiny but

the general attempt seems to be to *discredit* the Congress
Sub-committee's findings and to shift responsibility of an
outrage which cannot be denied to *Indian* shoulder—*The
Skin Game* with a vengeance. Speaking at a mass meeting
the other day, I said that what we Indians demanded was
reparation and not revenge; that we had the spiritual
force and vision that enabled us to transcend hate and
transmute bitterness into something that might mean
redemption both for ourselves and the British race; but
that freedom was the only true reparation for the agony
and shame of the Punjab.

Are you well? The specialists think that my heart
disease is in an advanced and dangerous state: but I
cannot rest till I stir the heart of the world to repentance
over the tragedy of martyred India . . .

With greetings to all my friends, I am, as ever,

Your
Pal and loving friend,
Sarojini Naidu

4. Below is the correspondence between Mr Montagu (through this secretary Mr Brown) and Sarojini Naidu that she refers to in the previous letter to Gandhiji. These stemmed from her speech on the Punjab tragedy (pg 191):

(FIRST LETTER TO MRS. NAIDU)
India Office,
Whitehall, S.W.1.
9th July, 1920

IMMEDIATE
MADAM,

I am directed by the Secretary of State for India to invite your attention to the report of a public meeting at Kingsway Hall on the 3rd June, published by the organisers of the meeting. You are reported therein (page 17) to have said: 'My sisters were stripped naked; they were flogged; they were outraged'. As you have made no correction, the Secretary of State is bound to assume that you were correctly reported.

Mr. Montagu finds it difficult to believe that anybody could for one moment have thought that such occurrences were possible; and he finds that these particular allegations do not occur in the Report of the Committee appointed by the Indian National Congress (to which you appeared to refer as the authority for them) or in the Evidence collected by that Committee; and nothing in that Report or Evidence justifies the allegation that Indian women were stripped naked, or flogged, or outraged.

Mr. Montagu has satisfied himself that the statements that women were stripped naked, or flogged, or outraged during the operation of Martial Law in the Punjab are of course absolutely untrue. He therefore requests you to withdraw immediately the charges which you are reported to have made publicly, and for which, if correctly reported, you alone appear to be responsible, and to give to your withdrawal the same publicity as was given to the original statements, or if you are prepared to maintain the accuracy of these specific charges, to produce justification for them. The Secretary of State reserves the right of publishing this letter, but before doing so, proposes to await your reply, up to Wednesday morning, the 12th July.

I am, Madam,
Your obedient Servant,
(signed) S. K. BROWN

(SECOND LETTER TO MRS. NAIDU)
India Office,
Whitehall, S.W.1.
10th July, 1920

MADAM,

Since the despatch of my letter to you yesterday, the attention of the Secretary of State has been called to statement No. 147 printed on p. 194 of the Report of the National Congress sub-Committee.

Having regard to the general objects of the meeting, to the case which you desired to make to your audience, and to the context of your remarks, the Secretary of State does not think that this charge can be the allegation which you had in mind. It is an allegation wholly unconnected with Martial Law procedure, made against Indian Police constables and not against what you described as 'Martial Authorities'. It is not specifically referred to in the Congress Report.

If, however, this allegation which does appear in the Report or the Evidence published by the Congress Sub-Committee, is the foundation of your statement, he asks you to make it clear, that you had no reason to make such a charge against any 'Martial Authority' and that you had in your mind only an allegation made against the subordinate police in the course of search for stolen property.

I am to add that paragraph 10 of the Government of India's despatch of 3rd May last in which enquiry is promised into such cases of alleged ill-treatment, obviously applies to this case. The Secretary of State has also, however, directed special enquiry into this matter, and hopes in due course to be in a position to state to the public the results of the enquiry.

I am, Madam,
Your obedient Servant,
(signed) S.K. BROWN

Sarojini Naidu's reply

Duke's Hotel
35, St. James's Place
S.W.1.
July 12th, 1920

To:
The Rt. Hon. E.S. Montagu
Secretary of State for India
India Office.

Dear Sir,

I am in receipt of the letters of the 9th and 10th inst., sent me by your Secretary at your direction.

I notice that the statements contained in the first letter are considerably modified in the second. While the first categorically denies the existence of any evidence published by the Congress Sub-Committee to justify the remarks made in my Kingsway Hall Speech to which you refer, the second on the contrary admits that there is such evidence, but that the outrages were the work of the police and not of Martial Law Authorities.

I am surprised that you should attempt to make such a fine distinction, the materiality of which is not obvious, when the police were an integral part of the Martial Law machinery and admittedly were serving the purposes of 'Martial Law Authorities' inasmuch as these outrages were perpetrated by them to procure evidence for the Martial Law Tribunals.

In any case, if you turn to my speech itself, the report of which is not entirely accurate, you will note that there are only two instances of outrage upon women which I have specifically attributed to Martial Law Authorities. These remarks were based upon several statements made by these women themselves, which read thus:

Statement 581, Page 866, Made by twenty-three women.

We were called from our houses or wherever we were and collected near the school. We were asked to remove our veils. We were abused and harassed to give out the name of Bhai Mool Singh as having lectured against the Government. This incident occurred at the end of Baishakh last in the morning in Mr. Bosworth Smith's presence. He spat at us, and said many bad things. He beat some of us with sticks. We were made to stand in rows and to hold our ears. He abused us also, saying 'Flies, what can you do if I shoot you?'

Passage from statement 362, Page 367

While the men were at the Bungalow, he rode to our village, taking back with him all the women who met him on the way carrying food for their men to the Bungalow. Reaching the village, he went round the lanes and ordered all women to come out of their houses, himself forcing them out with sticks. He made us all stand near the village Daira. The women folded their hands before him. He beat some with his stick and spat at them and used the foulest and most unmentionable language. He hit me twice and spat in my face. He forcibly uncovered the faces of all the women, brushing aside the veils with his own stick.

He repeatedly called us she-asses, bitches, flies and swine and said: 'You were in the same beds with your husbands; why did you not prevent them from going out to do mischief? Now your skirts will be looked into by the village constables.' He gave me a kick also, and ordered us to undergo the torture of holding our ears by passing our hands round the legs while being bent double.

This treatment was meted out to us in the absence of our men who were away at the Bungalow.

This statement was corroborated by eight other women who made similar statements.

Passage from statement 585, Made by Mai Caban, Page 869

On the 5th of Baishakh bullets were fired into our village. The village people ran away hither and thither. One European who was on horseback called some old women together and told them that whatever he had done (firing) was done well. The old women did not give any reply. He then abused them and beat them with a stick. He then asked other women to stand in a row. Those who had veiled their faces were forced to remove their veils. They too were beaten with sticks.

From Statement 125, Page 177

I am a purdahnashin. I never appear in public, not even before the servants. I was, however, called down from my house. I went with a purdah (veil). I was peremptorily ordered to take off my purdah. I was frightened and removed the purdah. I was then asked who assaulted Miss Sahib. They threatened me that unless I named the assailant, I would be given over to the soldiers.

Need I remind you that the purdah is as sacred to the Indian woman as is her veil to the Catholic nun, and forcibly to unveil an Indian woman constitutes in itself a gross outrage.

The other instances of outrage to which I draw attention in my speech, were not specifically attributed to any special individual. My charges, however, were based on statement 147, page 194, which, as you are aware, is of too indecent a nature to be quoted here or from the public platform.

I would further refer you to statements 130 and 131, which deal with the conduct of soldiers and not of the police.

I am deeply grieved to discover that until now you were not cognizant of the statements embodied in the Congress evidence concerning such outrages upon Indian women; and I trust that you are causing an exhaustive and impartial enquiry to be made into such cases.

Yours faithfully
SAROJINI NAIDU

II

Your Secretary's letter of August 24, enclosing at your direction the paraphrase of the Government of India's telegram has only just reached me on my return from the country, or I should have answered it earlier. I note that it has also been communicated to the Press, but apparently without being accompanied by the previous correspondence between us, which is essential to a proper understanding of the whole matter. I can hardly believe that the Government of India's telegram is seriously put forward as a refutation of charges of the gravest kind, based on the statements of witnesses whose evidence has been tested by cross-examination, and is published on the authority of a Committee consisting of distinguished and widely respected men, who are all members of the English Bar, one of whom has filled a high judicial office, and two of whom hold leading positions as practising lawyers in their respective Provinces; while the integrity of our friend Mr. Gandhi and his scrupulous care in such matters are as well-known to you as to me. If that is so, are we asked to accept a bare denial put forward by the Deputy Commissioner—an interested party—covered and confused by entirely irrelevant allegations, made obviously with a hope to discredit the unfortunate victims of conduct the revolting brutality of which cannot be qualified by the character of those subjected to it?

I am ashamed to think that a British official should suppose that such an atrocious charge could be lightly disposed of by such a callous and contemptible method as the suggestion that the people concerned are too degraded to have any claim on human credulity.

May I remind you that specific charges have been made of gross outrage on several women? I refer you to statement 147 of the Congress Committee's evidence. There is nothing in the Government of India's telegram which disposes of those charges.

The remark that 'The women stood in a public lane adjoining the Kotwali, or police station, where no public officer would dare to treat them indecently,' is preposterous in view of the terrorised condition of the populace throughout the period of martial law, and the acknowledged facts regarding every kind of outrage inflicted on individuals of all classes in public.

It is, moreover, a monstrous misrepresentation to say that 'It is common knowledge in India that low class women embroider their complaints in this fashion.' I am proud to believe that the most fallen Indian woman would recoil from the humiliation of being forced, except under dire necessity, to relate the story of such an odious outrage.

The further suggestion that such statements had been made from motives of revenge is not only unworthy and incredible, but is actually discredited by the Government of India's admission that no complaints were made at the time, and the fact that those charges only came to light where investigators whom they had no cause to fear were at work some months later.

I cannot conceive what relevance the final paragraph of the Government of India's telegram has to these charges, but it is interesting to learn that a judicial tribunal was in receipt of confidential reports concerning the persons whom it tried.

However satisfactory, so futile and dishonest an attempt to deal with grave charges might seem to General Dyer's friends and admirers inside and out of Parliament, I prefer to cherish a belief that it will not be so easily accepted by the public in this country, and it is certain that Indians who are chiefly interested in this question could not possibly accept unsupported denials either by officials or by the Government of India, whose record in regard to the sufferings of the people of the Punjab has deprived it of all title to their confidence in matters of this kind.

As for me, I shall be prepared to disbelieve those charges only when they have been conclusively disproved by a proper judicial inquiry. Am I to infer that you do not propose to direct the Government of India to hold such an inquiry? I fully understood that the term 'special inquiry 'in your letter of July 10 implied something more than a mere reference to the Deputy Commissioner. May I also draw your attention to the other charges equally grave made against a British officer by a very large number of women, and set out in detail in my letter to you of July 12. The Government of India's telegram does not deal with those at all, and I should be glad to learn what steps have been taken to ensure a thorough impartial investigation.

5. **Sarojini Naidu to Gandhiji**
    Johannesburg,
    29 February 1924

It is the still small hour when a really truthful person does not know whether to say good night or good morning, going on to about three o'clock. The whole of Johannesburg is profoundly asleep after its long day of toil and revel and for the moment it has doffed its usual daily garment of race conflict and race arrogance.

I cannot sleep in South Africa and it is all your fault. You haunt the land and its soil is impregnated with the memory of your wonderful struggle, sacrifice, and triumph. I am so deeply moved, so deeply aware all the time that here was the cradle of Satyagraha—do you wonder that I have been able to move thousands of men and women in the last two days to tears under the influence and stimulus of your inspiration? Something has come to me since I entered the Transvaal and the heart of the enemy, even while it dissents, melts between my hands as I speak, arraign and appeal . . . Scores and scores of Europeans have said since I arrived that they hope and believe that what they call my brave fight will triumph. I have no doubt of that victory—since the cause is yours, the battle yours, the soldier yours—and yours the ambassador to make peace but peace which shall be a victory and bought with a price . . .

I have seen your legion of old friends and followers— white, brown and black, the whole gamut of the polychromatic scale of humanity in this land—all send you their love, especially the Phillips and Hermann Kallenbach and others. How can I remember everyone who loves you? The Tamil women are very spry—they say, *'Hum Gandhi ke sath jail gaya tha. Phir bhi jayega agar tum bolo.'*

From the Transvaal I go to Cape Town, thence to Durban (of course to Phoenix) and I set my face homewards on the 16th and reach on 5th April. I shall of course fly swifter on my broken wing than any dove to see you and after that to the Golden Threshold for a day or two. Padmaja has sent me an enchanting description of you in your bed jacket of doubtful Swadeshi, sitting up in bed. The letter reached me as I sat down to a banquet and I read it out to an enchanted audience! I do hope you are getting to be a formidable rival to your lieutenant Shaukat Ali in physical force!! Wouldn't you love some Cape pears and peaches. I'll eat them on your behalf while I'm here and if I think they'll travel, well I'll bring some with me.

I think I must go to bed now—it is distinctly good morning, I'm afraid. I shall have hollows around my eyes tomorrow and look like a hag instead of the 'charming visitor' that the South African papers believe me to be! What a tragedy especially as I have to be photographed for Indian Opinion. Tell little Ba that I shall bring her the minutest details of her son. Padmaja has warned me that Ba expects a catalogue of items about him—body, soul, and mind.

May I confess very privately that at odd intervals I don't feel very Satyagrahi but am consumed with envy, malice and wrath because everyone is falling over his neighbour to get your 'darshan' and I am defrauded of my fair claim—that is arrogance on my part, is it not? But Padmaja and Mina will have their heads pinched for so basely stealing a march upon me and going off to see you the minute you had revived from chloroform!

However, I am on my pilgrimage which somehow has also become an embassy in the course of which I have delivered your epigram as an ultimatum 'within the empire if possible, without the empire if necessary'. Personally, my tendencies are all towards the latter portion of your saying.

Au revoir!
Sarojini Naidu

6. To Leilamani Naidu, her daughter

Le Grand Hotel
Marseille
4 March 1921

My beloved little child:

This is my last night in Europe, in this great foreign, arrogant continent where through my song and speech and struggle I have won a place for India. Now I am glad to set my face homewards once more to serve India with speech and song and struggle: the one poignant regret I have is that I leave you behind—alone. You—with your brave, beautiful, rebellious, ignorant youth; you—with your passionate, implacable temperament, so audaciously sure of itself, its aims, its innocence, its lofty ideals and lively desires and dreams, and yet so threatened with perils and pitfalls, all the more to be feared because you are so fearless, so impatient to tender counsel born of bitter experience . . . My little girl, how I have tried to shield and guard you, to save you from the suffering and disillusion arising out of your own too eager, too exacting demands upon friendships and affections and understandings, unused and unable to endure the strain of such fury and insistent demands . . . When you have resented what you thought was an attempt to curb and control and hamper you, I assure you my darling there was nothing but the purest, most deepest comprehending mother-love, trying to safeguard you from the results of your own impetuous and vivid nature and impulses—so harshly misjudged and misconstrued by even those who seemed to you most of necessity to understand an appreciate . . . It is because I want to protect you from suffering such as I had to endure in my youth because my temperament and ideas were different—*they are different from what the world accepts and understands*—*that I tried* to guide you . . . But as the French poet said, 'A *chacun son infini*'—and you must find and realise your own soul in the infinity of its own loneliness, my child. Only remember that you are an Indian girl and that puts upon you a heavier burden than if you were an English girl born to a heritage of freedom. Remember that you have to help India to be free and the children of tomorrow to be free-born citizens of a free land therefore—if you are true to your country's need you must recognise the responsibility of your Indian womanhood. Nothing in your speech or action should cause the progress of Indian women to suffer, nothing in yourself should give room for wretched reactionary slave-minds to say, 'This comes of giving too much education and freedom to our women.' Think over it my darling. You are not free—one is—in the sense of being a law unto yourself in defiance of all existing tradition in our country—for freedom is the heaviest bondage in one sense since it entails duties, responsibilities and opportunities from which slaves are immune . . . *Noblesse oblige*! and the ampler the liberty the narrower the right to do as one pleases. And you my friend of delight . . . you must shine as a foremost gem in the crown of India's freedom . . . You have in you all the seeds of true greatness: be great my little child, fulfil yourself nobly in accordance with all the profound and beautiful impulses and ideals of your nature . . . but always remembering that you are the symbol of India. And may God prosper you in all things. I love you my baby. You will never know how dearly, and with what anxious and yearning tenderness . . .

And now let me tell you of my holiday in Paris . . . from the moment I left London till this moment when I sit in Marseille with envy of the shore of the gay Provencal town, it has been delightful. In my compartment in the London train the lady who sat opposite me, married to a Romanian noble, had many common friends including the Romanian poetess Helene Vacareco. The lady at my side turned out to be the wife of the famous musician Landor Roland who is so anxious to compose some music for my work. On the boat a lady came and sat next to me who said, 'I can never forget your eyes—you are the Indian poet' and she turned out to be Countess Tolstoi, a niece of the great writer Tolstoi. In Paris I spent 2 exquisite days revisiting all my favourite places, churches, museums, parks, and palaces—I went and paid my devotions to the statue of Joan of Arc in the Pantheon where the great men of France are buried (the very first speech I made at 11 years of age was on Joan of Arc!), I visited the Theatre Sarah Bernhardt and saw the famous Guitry family act—what grace, what art, what distinction! I heard two unpublished songs of mine which were sung by a man who has won fame in two Continents. I wandered through old Paris, in the Latin Quarter famed in literature, the haunt of students, artists, poets, beggars! And saw and even took part in the blithe Mt Carmel festival that sends all Paris mad! The mid-day procession I watched from an upper window—a real mad-glad carnival of students and townsfolk, dressed in every sort of fantastic costume and cars decorated in different ways full of beautiful girls chosen from different parts of the city dressed in wonderful clothes and music of course, mad and merry! In the night I walked and walked and walked, pushed and jostled by the gay crowds all drunk with high spirits and youth and springtime gaiety. I was hit on the back with floral rods, clapped on the head with a tambourine and chucked under the chin by a roguish girl masquerading as sailor boy and I thoroughly enjoyed myself even though my feet nearly fell off with fatigue.

Such a carnival is impossible in sombre and splendid London! Paris is the source of gaiety, something in the air makes one young and adventurous and full of *joie de vivre*. How you would have loved the Mt Carmel and how glad I am to have had that brief, happy interlude before I take upon myself the grave problems and perplexities that await me in India.

Well, goodnight my little Papi and good bye!

You are the guardian of my Jewel of Delight . . . Beware! Be faithful to your trust and keep the treasure of your soul incorruptible.

Your,
Mother
My boat sails at noon tomorrow

7. **Sarojini Naidu to Nehru**
   Lucknow
   29 September 1929

My beloved Jawahar:

I wonder if in the whole of India there was yesterday
a prouder heart than your father's or a heavier heart
than yours. Mine was the peculiar position of sharing in
almost equal measure both his pride and your pain. I lay
awake until late into the night thinking of the significance
of the words I had used so often in reference to you,
that you were predestined to a splendid martyrdom.
As I watched your face while you were being given the
rousing ovation on your election, I felt I was envisaging
both the Coronation and the Crucifixion—indeed the
two are inseparable and almost synonymous in some
circumstances and some situations: they are synonymous
today especially for you, because you are so sensitive and
so fastidious in your spiritual response and reaction and
you will suffer a hundred-fold more poignantly than men
and women of less fine fibre and less vivid perception and
apprehension, in dealing with the ugliness of weakness,
falsehood, backsliding, betrayal . . . all the inevitable
attributes of weakness that seeks to hide its poverty by
aggressive and bombastic sound . . . However I have an
abiding faith in your incorruptible sincerity and passion
for liberty and though you said to me that you felt you
had neither the personal strength nor a sufficient backing

to put your own ideas and ideals into effect under the turmoils of so burdensome an office. I feel that you have been given a challenge as well as offered a tribute: and it is the challenge that will transmute and transfigure all your noblest qualities into dynamic force, courage and vision and wisdom. I have no fear in my faith.

In whatever fashion it is possible for me to help you or serve you in your tremendous and almost terrible task, you know you have but to ask . . . if I can give no more concrete help, I can at least give you full measure of understanding and affection . . . and though, as Khalil Gibran says, 'The vision of one man lends not its wings to another man', yet I believe that the invincible faith of one's spirit kindles the flame of another in radiance that illumines the world . . .

Your loving friend and sister,
Sarojini Naidu

8. **Sarojini Naidu to Nehru**
   The Mahatma's Camp
   Calcutta
   13 November 1937

My very dear Jawahar:

I am writing from the modern version of the Tower of Babel. The Little Man is sitting unconcernedly eating spinach and boiled marrow while the world ebbs and flows about him breaking into waves of Bengali, Gujarati, English and Hindi. Bidhan and his colleagues are in despair over his stubborn indocility as regards his health. He is really ill . . . not only in his brittle bones and thinning blood but in the core of his soul . . . the most lonely and tragic figure of his time . . . India's man of destiny on the edge of his own doom . . .

To you, the other man of destiny, I am sending a birthday greeting . . . It will not reach you in time because of intervening eyes that must scan your correspondence. I have been watching you these two years with a most poignant sense of your suffering and loneliness, knowing that it cannot be otherwise.

What shall I wish you for the coming year? Happiness? Peace? Triumph? All these things that men hold supremely dear are but secondary things to you . . . almost incidental . . . I wish you, my dear . . . unflinching faith and unfaltering courage in your *via cruces* that all must tread who seek freedom and hold it more precious than life . . . not personal freedom but the deliverance of a nation from bondage. Walk steadfastly and along that steep and perilous path . . . if sorrow and pain and loneliness be your portion. Remember Liberty is the ultimate crown of all your sacrifice . . . but you will not walk alone.

Your loving,
Sarojini

9. Sarojini Naidu to Rabindranath Tagore
Hyderabad, Deccan
12 August 1940

Greetings to you, Poet in whose verses flow rivers of ancient wisdom and perennial youth, latest among those whom the old mother of learning far way has chosen to honour with the highest tribute in her gift . . . We have been reading with infinite delight, your beautiful reply and acknowledgement. It is poetry and prophecy in one.

I do not know how many more years of physical life may be added to your fourscore so richly attained, so superbly sustained, but when your now fragile and delicate body become a handful of scented ashes retrieved from the sandalwood pyre, unlike us, you'll still be triumphantly alive and immortal, your words will be the ever-loving symbol and indeed, reality of you, your very self . . .

May I thank you or is it the gods that I should thank for the loveliness and enchantment of your genius. A poet whose words have given so exquisite a treasure to the world and in your own words brought honour to India— an exalted service that none but two or three have been able to perform in like measure though in other ways . . . But your service is unique and inimitable and India in her day of peace will remember and cherish it.

Your loving,
Sarojini Naidu

PS. Padmaja and Leilamani are somewhat unreasonable. They think Oxford should have created an entirely new and superb honour to bestow on you!

10. Sarojini Naidu to Gopal Krishna Gokhale
Hyderabad, Deccan
24 December 1914

Dear Mr Gokhale

I have no news of or from you for some time now and in spite of my own stern and unselfish prohibition to you, feel both aggrieved and anxious at your silence. I hope it means that you are so much better that you have no time to write instead of so much worse that you have not the strength, in which case of course the illness would have been blazoned abroad with the true journalistic flair for 'personal items' concerning the Great Ones of the earth.

I should have written myself but my own health is in a most unsatisfactory condition: daily attacks of fever and perennial attacks of people!—both of which in their excess play havoc as you know with one's time and temper, not to speak of one's constitution. I don't seem to see any very successful remedies against the onslaught of both men and mosquitoes for some time to come. Both have one thing in common: they can sting; but fortunately that species of men that approximates to the local mosquito I have left behind to poison the air of London—perhaps next week of Madras! (That is malicious of me but true!)

Here the men are ([illegible] in its vague sense) strange as it may sound of Hyderabad!, decent and kind only: they live and let live. I wonder if it is because they have no ambitions to be Leaders—'Our Leaders' as my boys

ironically call them. Now laugh: relax your solemn brain
and laugh—whole heartedly as I do at the mosquito—
like, malarial, malicious men who disturbed your peace,
not long ago!

Oh, we want a new breed of men before India can
be cleansed of her disease. We want deeper sincerity of
motive, a greater courage in speech and earnestness in
action. We want men who love this country and are full
of yearning to serve and succour their brothers and not
to further aid in their degradation by insincerity and
self-seeking. O how I hate shams and prejudices; how I
hate all sectarian narrowness, all provincial limitations
of vision and purpose, all the arrogant sophistries of
man-made divisions and differences; how tired I am to
death of the reiterated resolutions that have become
almost meaningless by lip repetition: uncorroborated
by the heart's conviction and unsustained by practical
action—all this stirs me more deeply just now because
of the coming national week. What a week of inspiration
it should be to all partaking in the various activities, if
only all those activities could be so co-ordinated and
realised as intrinsic parts of the same many-sided work of
progress: the radii of one unshifting centre.

One needs a Seer's Vision and an Angel's voice to be
of any avail. I do not know of any Indian man or woman
today who has those gifts in their most complete measure.

I was to have gone to Madras, or rather they made
up their minds at the various conference committees that
I must speak, and I would gladly have done so, striking

in my own way, humbly and sincerely, the very note of co-ordination, but my health makes it impossible (and not safe) for me to face the exertions and excitements of so many activities. But I do not regret my inability to be present at the conferences half so much as my inability to accept the invitation—how cordial, how touching and how generous [?] of the student world who were hoping to organise all sorts of things in my honour. The students and the women of Madras: the two sections of the nation which are to be my special concern in all my future work.

I am afraid your absence again this year from the Congress will be a source of great disappointment and rob of it much of its dignity and authority. But your health is of far more urgent importance than even the Congress.

When do you go to Delhi: will it not be too severe a climate for your health? Are you taking your own doctor with you? And does he think you are really well enough to face such an ordeal of work and weather?

Please write to me or ask one of your chelas to send me a line before you leave for Delhi.

My husband is exceedingly busy. For some time the talk of his going had been slack, but just now again there seems to be a move to get him sent to the front! I suppose he would have to go as some General's staff. Meanwhile I fear my health causes him more anxiety than a whole field hospital full of (the) wounded is likely to cause him! He sends you or rather entrusted me some time ago with a message of most anxious good wishes for your speedy

recovery. My children send you their respects. They think
you must be a phenomenally wise and venerable person
because I always speak of you with so much, shall I say
respect or shall I say affection? Perhaps both would be
true: but that does not prevent me from taking you to
task when you are unwise and unvenerable enough to do
foolish things that hurt your health. I am always guilty
of such folly, but my children never suffered from any
illusion about my wisdom and venerable qualities: I am
their Pal and Comrade and fellow sinner in all things
human and delightful.

Remember me to your daughter and to your sister
also. And send me a potent Brahminical charm against
the ills of flesh—and the wars of my spirit!

Your affectionately,
Sarojini Naidu